[re]inventing the brand

can top brands survive the new market realities?

jean-noël **kapferer**

First published in French by Éditions d'Organisation in 2000
First published in English by Kogan Page Limited in 2001
Translated by Anglia Translations

Kogan Page
120 Pentonville Road
London N1 9JN
UK

Kogan Page
22 Broad Street
Milford CT 06460
USA

British Library Cataloguing in Publication Data

A CIP record for this book is available from the British Library.

ISBN 0 7494 3593 3

Typeset by Saxon Graphics Ltd, Derby
Printed and bound in Great Britain by Clays Ltd, St Ives plc

contents

Preface

The new realities of branding

Is current brand thinking obsolete? What is out of date in the classic rules of brand management that drive so many present-day marketing decisions? What emerging trends, perhaps already practised by some far-sighted and well-advised companies worldwide, will define brand management in the future? These are some of the questions addressed in this new book.

It is time to question the basic thinking behind brand management. It was created in different market conditions, different situations, and has been re-diffused time after time in brand management textbooks. Strategic wisdom warns: if it is taught, then it is probably obsolete; since the essence of good brand management is differentiation, advanced brand management should break free from the classic brand management moulds or at least not hesitate to question their relevance.

Market realities of this new millennium create a profound challenge. What are these realities that have created a radically new competitive market environment for branding decisions?

One is a shift in *distribution power*. Some multiple retailers (Wal-Mart, Ahold, Carrefour) represent purchasing volumes larger than those of many countries. They have developed sophisticated branding, and offer a full portfolio of their own-label brands, pushing many established brands off the shelf. This, in turn, leads to the need for a wider umbrella, or for source brands to host a wider array of products. Is it the end for P&G's sacrosanct product-brand model?

Another new reality is the rise of *consumer power*. Thanks to the Internet, it has often been said that consumers are gaining more power in their transactions, or their relationships with corporations and brands on the Web. This is true. But what then should brands do about this? Moreover, there are other factors to consider in the changing consumer market:

- The Internet revolution has started to shape new customer and consumer behaviours and has raised consumers' expectations of brands and corporations.
- We now live in post-modern societies where consumer fragmentation is the rule. We are moving away from markets made up of aggregated individuals; markets are now made up of networked consumers, communities and groups, but with what effect on branding?
- We also live in a global world, which, paradoxically, has stimulated some degree of craving for local identity. What should be the consequences for the 'global brand' religion?
- In Europe at least, consumers have had to face a number of food crises: from BSE, chicken flu or the GM crisis. The basis of trust has been shaken. Since trust is a key dimension of brand capital, brands need to respond to this loss of trust.
- In our modern societies, the ageing of the population means that brands will need to serve a larger number of generations altogether. This creates new demands, demands that are so far unmet.
- Our modern multi-channel environment has largely fragmented the media, calling into question the classic role of advertising in building brand loyalty and commitment.

How do these factors affect the basis of branding? What new contracts will form the basis of the brands of tomorrow (whether they are manufacturers' or distributors' brands)?

The milestone year 2001 seemed an appropriate time to reassess the situation and suggest new marketing strategies for brands seeking to gain or to preserve their market leadership. It is time to reinvent brand leadership.

part one

A new contract for the brands of the future

one

Convergence of brand cultures

'Brand' is a deceptively simple concept. Everyone can immediately come up with an example of a typical brand, but very few people are able to propose a satisfying definition: it is as if any definition that came to mind would not be complete. Some people talk about the name by which a product is known, others about added value, image, expectation, values, still others about the differentiating mark of the product and consumer badge. In fact, they are all right in their own way – a brand is all of these things simultaneously. There is no brand without a product, a mark and an image (collective representation). The brand is both the part and the whole; it is the mark on the product or service, but it is also the overall value conveyed with promises of tangible and intangible satisfaction.

The complexity of the concept of brand means that we cannot be hasty or simplistic when making statements about it. Moreover, the reality of the modern brand makes us realize that there are different types of brand. Hence the endless wrangling that conceals the fact that in reality, no one is talking about precisely the same thing. For the late Forrest Mars, brand was the name of his famous chocolate bar. For the chairman of Sony, it is the symbol of quality and progress in communications. In fact, there are two main brand cultures, based on the Western and the Japanese view of brand.

The cultures of East and West

Implicitly, all Western thinking about brands has been shaped by companies such as Procter & Gamble and Mars. These companies were created and flourished because they had products with something extra, and advertising enhanced their fame and image. They were the epitome of product branding. The management concepts that stem from this are the result of these origins. The key word is differentiation. The brand is here to differentiate between two products or services; it is part of an approach that carves up and segments the market. Ideally, each new segmentation should give rise to a new brand. The keywords here are targeting and positioning (comparative perception in relation to competitors from whom we wish to differentiate ourselves).

In Japan, nothing is more foreign to brand culture than this endless division. Fundamentally, the Japanese like names which, rather than dividing, separating and splitting, have the opposite function – that of grouping, encompassing, pooling resources, creating links. It is therefore unlikely that the phrase *brand stretching* has an equivalent in Japanese. Indeed, it would not cross the director of Yamaha's mind to use different brand names for its motorcycle business and its classical piano business. The more high quality, famous products there are worldwide under the Yamaha name, the greater the value of the name and the greater the pride felt by its employees. The Japanese have created a brand culture directly inspired by their notion of the company (Macrae, 1996).

Moreover, the world-famous Japanese brands are very often the names of groups – Mitsubishi, Sony, Toshiba, Matsushita, etc. In Japan, the reputation of the company comes before the reputation of the product. Until recently, this was not the case in the West, apart from in the business-to-business world. In fact, two consumer behaviour models are at work here:

- *The West works on the model of appropriation of the product.* This is why the identity of the product is packed with non-material elements. The brand evaluation criteria are differentiation, relevance, ego-enhancement.
- *Japan works on the loyalty model.* The important thing here is to build trust based on one name and one name only. The name of the company is the best candidate for the position of brand name, as it personifies power, continuity and status. Here, the source effect is critical; brand identity does not come from the

difference between brands, but from the key values that inspire the company. The word 'corporate' derives from 'corpus', the Latin for body. Brand identity in Japan results from an inward-looking approach, where what is important is not an obsession with the other, but respect for one's own values. We can therefore see how nothing could be more foreign to Japanese brand philosophy than Procter & Gamble's breakdown into standalone products (Ivory, Crest, Tide, Ariel, and so on), where they are almost ashamed of mentioning the parent company.

In the West, the origin of the brand was a creation for the consumer; the company was of concern only to Wall Street. Furthermore, every product had to have a brand. In Japan, reputation is indivisible, much like a human being, who is simultaneously a consumer, a citizen and an employee, hence the focus on umbrella brand policies, which are large, all-encompassing and draw their strength from their scale. It must be noted that today this practice is now being developed by product brand devotees. Mars has finally acknowledged the virtues of umbrella branding, and we can now find, depending on the country, ice creams, chocolate bars and an instant drink powder in addition to the famous Mars bar, all under the Mars name. It is true that having built such a reputation on the Mars name, yet deriving profit from just the chocolate bar, suddenly seemed wholly inappropriate to the management and shareholders of the famous company. The day will also come when there will be various forms of Ariel other than liquid, solid, micro or tablet, but for coloureds and wool. A name is either a by-word for quality or it isn't.

The rise of the company

We cannot ignore the fact that the Japanese model has now established itself in the West and vice versa. Western companies such as Unilever and P&G now display their name directly on advertisements for their products on Asian television channels. This is particularly noticeable, as we shall see later, in the rise of house brands, master brands, in references to the company on packaging and also in advertisements. A preoccupation with shareholders may have something to do with this – it is true that Wall Street places a higher value on companies that are well known, or whose brands are well known.

This increasing reference to the company comes in the context of a desire to give more meaning and depth to business. Making business emanate from a corporate body reassures the public in these insecure times (in the case of food, for instance), and also acknowledges the role of the community within the company, whose efforts and enthusiasm help make the brand possible. There has perhaps been too much of a tendency for the brand to hide the company, making it little more than a back office. Let's not forget that the brand originated in the know-how of the company. The launch of Saturn, a new American *marque* of car, in 1990, marked the beginning of the return of the company. Rather than merely presenting stereotypical images of cars and smug owners/drivers, the advertisements took the viewer round the factory, and showed the workers talking about their lives and the brand.

Convergence

Curiously, just as the West is rediscovering the company, the East is taking on board product brands and the segmentation of brand portfolios. Japanese companies have recognized that in some markets, there is a need to stimulate appropriation desires. The major Japanese car manufacturers have given their models fancy names – Celica, Civic, Corolla, etc – and these names are surprisingly enduring. They have even recognized the merits of segmentation by brand; Toyota has created a separate brand, Lexus, for its luxury cars, Honda launched the Accura, Nissan the Infinity.

However, the convergence of the two models also has an effect at the level of management methods and concepts. All brands now ask themselves questions about their 'mission', their 'raison d'être', their vision, their core values, all of which are terms straight out of business management. Brands are managed like virtual companies, and every company wants to be a brand, ie to inject meaning into their products and services. And this is what post-modern consumers expect.

Vertical and transverse brands

One of the striking features of the beginning of the new millennium is the power of vertical brands such as Gap, Zara and IKEA. Are they pleasant locations and stores, products, functions, experiences, sensations, images? They are surely all of these. On their own territory, brands reign supreme; when we go to Gap or Zara, we are entering their world.

Moreover, the ideal for the supermarkets is also to become the 'shop of their brand', whereas they are currently merely distributors of their private label and other brands. Décathlon is on the verge of succeeding in this goal – every Décathlon superstore is a Niketown in all but name. Décathlon is no longer just a store: it's even been called Disneycathlon. Décathlon realized that it had to be more than a shop, and turn itself into a leisure destination, a sort of mini-Disneyland dedicated to sport and fun. Every visit is an experience rather than simply the act of purchasing, built around what is poised to become, through the range of its offering, one of the only truly multi-sport brands in the market.

Generally, as they do not have to defend a legitimacy linked to the product or the know-how, retailers have discovered the virtues of transverse brands. No manufacturer could have created the brand now sold in the Carrefour group: Reflets De France. However, this is real value creation – grouping together all the products (almost a hundred) that make up the reputation of the regions of France and traditional flavours under one banner. This is extremely practical for the consumer, and very easy to identify on the shelves. The experiment is to be repeated in the extension of an organic brand, or a brand (Destination Saveurs) that groups together the best exotic products, where the consumer has no point of reference and expects a real service. The retailer is in a unique position to link up hundreds of independent producers with millions of consumers, the point of intersection being a reference brand. In so doing, he adds an undeniable value as the middleman, and the marketer of that brand.

Manufacturers are also becoming involved in brand extension through programme brands, which are not restricted to a single product. What is Nesquik's programme: to help mothers get their children to drink milk. Why limit Nesquik to just a chocolate drink? The Nesquik range now covers sweets, snack bars, chocolate bars, cereals, a milk-based dessert, etc. The common feature of all of these products is the combination of chocolate and milk – breakfast cereals need milk, there is milk in yogurt, and so on.

Multi-parent brands

When they are not stand-alone (ie simple product brands), brands are generally the offspring of just one parent. Thus, we talk about Danone's Bio, or Lu's Petits Ecoliers. But when the Danone group wants to make its low-fat Taillefine (in English 'slim waist') range a programme brand, we have to recognize that depending on the product category, Taillefine will have different parents – Danone in the refrigerated products section for low-fat yogurts or mineral water, but Lu for low-fat biscuits and nibbles. We are therefore seeing a new type of brand, daughter brands that have two different mothers. This is a new structure, and is the result of the vertical culture of the legitimacy of the manufacturer's brands; Lu specializes in biscuits and dry foods, but not in refrigerated products. So how is the added value shared between the different actors? How do consumers find their bearings in this new family unit?

Generally speaking, there has been a considerable increase in co-branding and co-parenting – Danone and Minute Maid, Nestlé and Coca-Cola, Mattel and Compaq. The approach draws its strength from the complementary nature of each brand's attributes and is an alternative to brand stretching. In this way it avoids the problems of each brand's lack of legitimacy when it is taken in isolation away from its area of competence. The partner brands create value by combining their respective skills.

two

Unveiling the company behind the brand

In 1998, an event occurred that was symptomatic of the changes taking place in the world of brand marketing. Breaking with a long-standing tradition of individual brand marketing, and capitalizing on the reputation of such big names as Plénitude, Elnett and Progress, the French cosmetics company L'Oréal decided to display its name prominently on all products of these brands and their related communication. It did this by using a parent brand (L'Oréal Paris), a common slogan – 'car je le vaux bien' (because I'm worth it) – and the same promotional style. In so doing, it put an end to a tradition that was regarded as untouchable: stand-alone brands.

Other companies have adopted the same approach: some a long time ago, most more recently. Thus, although the Coca-Cola Company manages an extremely diverse brand portfolio, it nevertheless reminds consumers that all its products have been produced by Coca-Cola. For example, Fanta – Coca-Cola's world-famous orange-flavoured drink – carries a clear indication on the front of the can that it is 'a product of the Coca-Cola Company'. There is nothing discreet about it, not like Procter & Gamble's star logo which appears at the bottom or on the back of its products.

Nestlé has recently begun to put its seal of guarantee on most of its products, even Herta pork meat products, although it does not appear on Perrier, Vittel or Friskies. In 1998, Accor launched an international campaign centred around its 'smiling image' logo which is now prominently displayed at the entrance to all its hotels, whatever their brand is.

These examples illustrate an underlying trend that is well worth looking at more closely. This is not corporate communication in the true sense, ie a reference to the 'corpus' (corporate entity) of the company, its operation and results. In fact, several companies that have adopted this approach have continually emphasized that their aim is not to engage in corporate publicity, preferring to be discreet about their business affairs, especially if they are not quoted on the Stock Exchange. Basically what is happening is the creation of a 'supra brand' that uses the name of the company.

So why do products need a 'supra brand' name? Interestingly, the German term is 'eine Dach-Marke' (roof brand) while an alternative English term is 'house brand', as if the usual brand structure were no longer enough without a roof or, which amounts to the same thing, without a global reminder of the house (company) to which it belongs.

It is worth noting that the actual definition of 'brand' contains a dichotomy charged with implications: a name, sign or symbol that identifies the origin of a particular group of products or services and differentiates them from those of competitors. This legal definition attests to the two basic structural functions of a brand: to identify the origin of an item and differentiate it from other brands. Until recently all Western branding ideology was dominated by the logic of differentiation, a concept already examined in the comparison of East–West brand cultures (see Chapter 1). For example, in the washing-powder marketing manuals, the role of the brand has traditionally been to make each washing powder look different and special in the eyes of consumers in spite of their apparent similarity. The same principle was applied to soft drinks. However, the limits of this approach appear to have been reached.

The function of source, which has long been underestimated, has become a key issue in competitivity in the 21st century. Companies are experiencing the need to use what psychologists refer to as the 'source effect', the key credibility factor in persuasive communication. The source-brand doesn't differentiate, it gives credibility, authenticity, offers a guarantee, is a sign of power, expertise and ethics. Eight basic trends explain this pressing need to use the 'source effect' leverage when creating a supra brand. Let's consider each one in turn.

Distribution: maximizing the 'power effect'

To say that distribution is now becoming concentrated in the hands of a few companies is an understatement. At national, European and international level, the number of players is decreasing to the advantage of a small number of groups which are becoming increasingly concentrated and powerful. In many cases, three distribution groups often account for 65 per cent of brand sales on the mature European markets. At the present rate of development, this will soon apply to Brazil or Taiwan, as anyone who visits these countries will realize. The leading European distribution groups and Wal-Mart have successfully exported there the concept of the superstore. In Europe, the recent merger of Carrefour and Promodès means that these two distributors now completely dominate the Spanish and Portuguese markets.

It should be noted that the mass multiple retailers certainly know how to give a show of strength. The distribution groups tend to take the name of their flagship company. In fact, Promodès was in the process of changing its name to Groupe Continent, the name of its leading international hypermarket chain, just before it took the plunge and amalgamated with Carrefour.

What weight do the various brands of a company's brand portfolio actually carry on the shelves? The leading brands are certainly recognized as such. A company's first response to the concentration of distribution is to further strengthen its strongest brand through advertising, innovation and direct contact with consumers. But what about the other brands? Today companies feel the need to link their brands and products via a common thread or red ribbon. This doesn't mean creating an umbrella brand (a type of brand name covering several product categories), but a unifying brand, a link whose scope acts as a reminder that behind a particular product or products lies another force, a guarantee, a source of confidence.

It is a question of flexing the muscles that the multiplication of segmented and compartmentalized brands might have concealed. For example, behind Plénitude, Progress and Elnett lies L'Oréal. The target groups in this type of initiative are the shelf managers, the person in charge of the product category at distribution level and, thirdly, the consumer.

In some sectors, there is a difficulty in implementing this strategy. The strength of a company is measured by the strength of its brands. Logically, therefore, all that company's energy and financial investment should be channelled into developing these brands. In that case, how does it develop the status of the common thread, the parent brand or the supra brand that has become so vital?

The cheese sector provides a good illustration of the problem. As well as their recognized leading brands, companies in this sector also have a wide range of specialist products and less-well-known product brands. For example, the Leerdammer brand and its many extensions are well known throughout continental Europe. However, not many people have heard of Baars, the company that produces and promotes Leerdammer as well as a number of speciality cheeses. Baars feels the need to link its products via a common sign or marque.

Packaging is an obvious way of doing this. So Baars displays its name discreetly on the packaging of all its cheeses, unlike Kraft which labels all its European cheeses very prominently. In France, Bel's red logo appears on all its cheeses – from Vache-Qui-Rit to Rouy, Cousteron and Sylphide – but unobtrusively so as not to interfere with their individual identity. However, reputations are not built on the basis of the stalactite effect or, if they are, it is a very slow process. This raises the issue not only of a more direct form of promotion, but also of how to achieve this without diverting investment from the brands.

One way is to capitalize on the company name. Kraft is the first part of the company name KJS, while Baars is Leerdammer's producer. But since there isn't a cheese called Baars, the company has been tempted to promote its name at least on the side of its trailers that travel the length and breadth of Europe. But wouldn't it be better to leave them as they are, ie with a huge slice of Leerdammer on public view, to further reinforce the brand image?

Playing the loyalty card

Today, loyalty is a buzzword. The preoccupation with volume and market share only makes sense if it is profitable. Hence marketing efforts target the customers with the greatest profit potential, whose loyalty should be further increased. But distributors also try to develop loyalty to their outlets by, among other things, offering a wide range of distributor's brands. Hence the need to break down the distribution barrier and communicate directly with the best customers of the company's brands.

Given the cost of implementing such a strategy (over 20 million euros for such major marketers as French food giant Danone), there is a need to share these costs. This has led to the creation of horizontal marketing initiatives, a joint venture by all the brands of a particular company aimed at achieving maximum exposure and efficiency. This may involve the creation of a customer database like the one created by Danone which, at the end of 1999, comprised almost 2.8 million households, major consumers of the group's brands.

It may involve the creation of a joint Web site or the mounting of joint promotional initiatives, like the Nestlé breakfast campaign.

But to return to the example of Baars in the Netherlands, what do you call these horizontal marketing initiatives? You can't call them Leerdammer or give them a more generic name such as 'the cheese board'. You have to use a supra name. Danone capitalizes on its company name (which is also the name of its most famous brand) by using the Danoé name for the consumer magazine. Accor has made use of this synergy by giving its group name to one of its products. The former stand-alone brands Africa Tours, Asia Tours and America Tours have been brought together under a single name: Accor Tours. To have a product in the range that bears the name of the group provides additional leverage in establishing its reputation.

Client concentration

Globalization is not limited to the distribution sector. Buyers are also becoming 'global' which is increasing their power in the marketplace. Accor has global contracts with IBM for services which guarantee the mobility of its executives at international level. Global buyers want global contacts and, in the first analysis, the brand name is for them irrelevant: Sofitel, Novotel, Mercure,

Europcars. They deal at the corporate level – generally speaking, the more fragmented the clientele, the more it favours accessible, local contacts. The more global the clientele, the more it wants to deal at corporate level. In the United States, for example, Schneider Electric uses its local company brand name, Square-D, to represent the group at national level. At international level, ie in all other countries, the group is known under its corporate brand name: Schneider Electric.

The risk society

In certain markets, and especially the food market, there is an increasing sense of mistrust. Insofar as everything that is ingested bears an intrinsic and potentially life-threatening risk, consumers are naturally sensitive to any hint of danger linked to the major food brands. Recent events have taken these fears one step further by exteriorizing them: the BSE crisis, chicken flu, the withdrawal of certain mineral waters and cans of Coca-Cola, the tussle between the United States and Europe over the hormone content of US veal exports. Not to mention the emotionally charged issue of the fundamental changes to modern civilization in the form of GM foods. In fact, we are well and truly embroiled in a risk society. The recent cases listed above represent a catalogue of failures in the control systems and regulatory procedures implemented at company and government level. In an open society, opposition groups, counter-powers, will make increasing use of the risk factor (the slightest potential for danger) and bring it to public attention via media debates, and e-lobbying.

The problem lies in the fact that brands only envisaged the risks from the point of view of what could be called a market model. They targeted consumers in the purest and strictest sense of the term, whereas the recent conflicts are a sign of the citizen's involvement in the market sector. While the latter adopts a holistic, global and generalized approach to things, brands focus only on the desires and possibly the well-being of the consumer. But what of the identity and civil liberties of the ordinary man and woman in the street? Who will speak about those?

This raises the problem of the type of sender needed. Couldn't the 'fun' food brands also be used to reassure people? It is doubtful. The house brand has a role to play in presenting the responsible side of the company and the values on which it will not compromise. Confidence is certainly boosted by a demonstration of the efforts made to minimize the risk, but also of the shared values that form the guiding principle of action, ahead of economic considerations and profitability, beyond a mere market model.

The fears of ordinary consumers must be addressed first and foremost through actions: for example, what is actually being done to ensure quality? But transparency is also important. With processes and products high on the agenda, the need for traceability in the food sector is paramount. It is vital for consumers to regain control of their lives by knowing exactly what they are buying. Labelling, indications of origin and symbols representing the non-use of certain types of processing, must be more widely used alongside the actual brand names. Transparency in communication is also important, for example the development of information forums on the Internet.

At brand level, there will therefore be increasingly less tolerance of stand-alone brands since they tend to exacerbate consumer fears by making frivolous if not outrageous claims. In psychoanalytical terms, the more a brand releases the subconscious and the impulses, the more it requires a counterweight, a superego. This is the role of the supra brand, which may be the corporate brand.

In the food sector, the trend towards multi-level-branding has already begun. Nestlé displays its name on Lion, Nuts and Kit-Kat bars, which makes it possible to operate on two levels: desire and reassurance.

It should be noted that this trend goes far beyond the food sector. For example, there is a strong need for security and reassurance in the car sector where niche brands such as Saab and Alfa-Romeo use the backing of General Motors and Fiat. Similarly, Redland tiles use the backing of Lafarge, and Banque Directe of Bnp-Paribas.

The rise of the opinion formers

One of the consequences of this growing concern is the increased effect of opinion formers and influencers on the choices made by end-users. Doctors, dieticians and researchers are often asked for their opinion on a particular product, ingredient or brand. It is no longer possible to ignore these opinion leaders. Even Vichy, which specializes in OTC cosmetic dermatology, has decided to conduct a campaign of systematic information for dermatologists. The company does not expect them to actively prescribe Vichy products since these are produced for the mass market and are not classified as 'curative'. However, it is impossible for a leading cosmetic-dermatology brand not to maintain regular contact with dermatologists, if only to keep them informed of the latest advances and avoid negative recommendations.

The brand therefore has to maintain two dialogues. The first is an imaginative, idealized and euphoric advertising dialogue aimed at consumers. The second – more serious, factual, well documented and socially responsible – is aimed at the press, government departments and consumer groups. Credibility is crucial at this second level. For brands such as Évian, whose message is based on health, there is less of a discrepancy between the two levels of communication. However, smaller brands that do not have the status of Évian and Vichy will lack credibility when trying to communicate to the opinion leaders. The supra brand makes this role easier, especially if it conveys responsibility and credibility by using the corporate name. For example, it is Danone that provides information on Actimel and Bio, not the individual brand marketing.

The globalization of business

The supra brand is also a response to increased competition. The globalization of business should in fact make companies more modest. In the Vivendi group, for example, each sector has its own master brand: Cégétel (telephones), Onyx (waste disposal and processing), Connex (transport). The question arises as to whether in other countries, say China or the United States, these should be presented as Onyx (Vivendi group) or simply as Vivendi, even though this means subsequently calling upon each specialist sector.

In fact, the successful launch of Vivendi in 1999 has created a new, ready-to-use resource via the kudos associated with the corporate name at international level. Why continue to approach foreign markets as it was historically done in the domestic market? Since a supra brand has been created, why not use it? The creation of Vivendi Water, under the banner of Vivendi Environment, has done just that.

This logic is particularly relevant for groups that have been formed progressively, from the top down, and have brought together companies with a reputation in their own particular sector. Initially, it was standard practice to capitalize on the brands that had a reputation in their specialist field and were well known to the technical decision makers. In this way, the Schneider group (now Schneider Electric) capitalized on the names of Merlin-Gérin and Télémécanique which were famous names in the engineering sector. But, outside its traditional markets, it reverses the process by adopting an approach that focuses on the corporate brand as the only source of value and basis for its reputation. Here it is Schneider that has a reputation as a specialist and integrator on the world markets, even though it has to fall back on its specialist brands: Square-D, Télémécanique, Merlin-Gérin and Modicon. Furthermore, as major international contracts involve an increasing number of non-technicians in the decision-making processes (eg politicians), they find the name of the corporation more reassuring.

In a completely different market, the toy market, manufacturers of traditional domestic brands are having to adapt their management model and approach foreign markets under a single banner, with a single catalogue and standardized packaging. This is why the Berchet group has been created, bringing the brands Berchet, Charton, Favre, Clairbois and ToysToys together under the Berchet group supra brand. This was the only way to compete with Mattel.

Concentration of resources

The visible emergence of the corporate brand also meets the need to give a name to the common process shared by different brands, especially if this common ground is becoming a growing reality. The car industry is a good example.

Brands, which were originally individual companies, have been gradually bought up by groups such as General Motors, Ford, Volkswagen, PSA Peugot Citroën, and Fiat. As a result of these mergers and takeovers, the companies have regrouped their resources. For example, PSA is no longer the simple financial holding it once was. PSA and General Motors include a range of departments, from R&D through purchasing, logistics and finance to human resources and production. Their factories are no longer devoted to a particular brand but to common platforms for different brand models. Brands are responsible for planning the products of the future, design, 'typing' cars as a function of the distinctive positioning attributes of the brand, marketing and commercialization. Now, who announces the latest major innovation? Usually it is the entity that has produced it, before it is subsequently developed by one or other of the group's brands. In the United States, it is General Motors; in France, PSA. However the limitations of this exercise are obvious since, while GM has an international reputation and therefore operates as a supra brand, PSA does not. There aren't any PSA cars and there aren't likely to be. Furthermore, in the face of outside competition, every effort should be made to strengthen the image of the Peugeot and Citroën brands. In this respect, there is no point in using the group name too visibly if this reduces the impact of the announcement of an innovation attributed to one or other of the two brands. However, in many countries where Peugot or Citroen are just starting to develop, there is a very strong resistance to stand-alone 'orphan' brands and people generally like to know that a relatively unknown brand has the backing of a better-known group. One way of solving these contradictory requirements is to give the supra brand the name of one of the brands in its portfolio, while taking great care to distinguish between the two (brand and group) levels. This is the solution chosen by the Volkswagen group, the Ford, Daimler-Chrysler group and the Fiat group.

Although this strategy has also been adopted by PSA Peugeot Citroën, being too long the name is unfortunately all too often reduced to the PSA acronym.

Shareholder involvement

Today the shareholder or rather the shareholders are very much in the spotlight. It is because they are so numerous and often fragmented that brand policies also try to influence market valuation. The former Rhône Poulenc group transferred its chemical sector to a subsidiary which it called Rhodia in order to bring the Rhône Poulenc share price closer to the standards of the pharmaceutical industry. Until then the market had shown a below-par rating due to the presence of the chemical sector under the same name. As soon as the name Générale Des Eaux was replaced by Vivendi in 1999, the market valuation increased by 20 per cent.

Stock-exchange evaluators assess companies in the light of two criteria. They require them to have:

- a simple strategy;
- transparent communication (here 'communication' is understood in the broadest sense of the term).

In January 2000, the Vivendi group not only established its environmental sector as a company in its own right, but also as a brand with its own logo. The aim was to have it quoted on the Stock Exchange and, in so doing, provide a response to the financial critics who no longer look favourably upon overly diversified conglomerates.

From their point of view, single brands or clearly identified master brands are preferable. It may be good to be a group with a range of different brands, but it's even better to have a reputation in your own right. Hence the value of displaying the company name, even in small lettering, on its products. The visibility of the name is one of the immaterial leverages that influence the share price.

Citizen power

The Coca-Cola crisis in June 1999 in Europe (with suspicion on the manufacturing process of cans) marked an increase in citizen power and the disarray of consumer-orientated companies in the face of such a crisis. This was certainly true of Coca-Cola, and indeed of most other companies. The issue raised by the crisis was not so much the health aspect as the loss of control over everyday life, ie the loss of freedom. A number of food crises have highlighted the failure of the so-called consumer protection agencies. Each new incident raises the spectre of a series of abdications of individual responsibility, at all levels in these agencies. At the same time, and exacerbated by the phenomenon of concentration, the range of real choice, and therefore freedom of choice, is reduced. Coca-Cola as a company could be called 'Micro-Soft Drink Ltd'. The avowed aim of its directors is to 'neutralize' competition. In all sectors, what is known as vertical integration in fact aims to recreate private monopolies, as seen in the communications sector, through the takeover of 'content' companies (films, programmes, publishing companies) by 'information' companies (telephone, Internet, television, information technology) such as in the Vivendi Universal or AOL–Time Warner cases. It is therefore possible to be extremely satisfied with the Coca-Cola product but increasingly uncomfortable with the company. The same applies to Windows and Microsoft.

One is a great software, the second is a de facto monopoly.

Until now, companies have relied on setting up foundations or charity programmes, or making donations (eg to the World Wide Fund for Nature), to manage their reputation vis-à-vis citizens. But the citizen hidden in each consumer is beginning to question the exact purpose of the companies behind the brands. Company communication must take account of this new demand, which idealized brand advertising is quite unable to meet. Generally speaking, companies will have to become more 'real' than they are at present.

three

From risk to desire: what functions for what brands?

The rise of distributors' brands in all sectors of the economy has fired a warning shot across the bows of the very concept of 'branding'. From a legal point of view, a 'brand' is an instrument for the protection of companies rather than consumers. Its optional nature makes it an instrument that companies may or may not decide to use to guarantee their exclusive rights on a sign. It should, however, be recognized that it doesn't appear to be particularly effective in protecting companies, hence the reliance on government bodies to regulate markets and control the relations between commerce and industry, when it is seen to be too imbalanced in favour of the former.

If brands, or at least certain brands, no longer provide effective leverage in ensuring a company's competitiveness and protection, it is because they have lost the prerogative of their function vis-à-vis the consumer. Brands acquire value in the eyes of the consumer because they fulfil certain functions, and a value is put on these functions depending on the type of consumer, product category and purchasing situation. The functional approach of brands sheds a light on the present and likely future situation of brands.

The main function of brands is to reduce perceived risk. As soon as a purchasing situation involves risk, the consumer naturally seeks to reduce that risk. There are several types of perceived risk. It may be financial, hence the increased importance of the brand when the price increases. It may be physical, hence the need for reassuring brand names in the food sector, where recent events highlighted the weaknesses in public regulatory bodies. This also explains the almost magical attachment of consumers to a particular brand name of aspirin. The name of the brand is associated with the psychological guarantee of relieving their headache, which is why generic products are only successful if they have the backing of national medical authorities (the FDA in the United States, the BMA in Great Britain) or are officially recommended by pharmacists if not made compulsory by private health insurances. Perceived risk also increases with technological advances and consumers look to such established brands as Sony or Thomson when it comes to introducing innovations in the field of digital and interactive television and stereo equipment. Finally, brands also respond to a perceived psychological risk. In fact, we wear far more brands than we consume, hence the omnipresent brand names in perfume, cosmetics, sport, watches, spectacle frames and so on. Brands have badge value in many categories.

The second function of brands is to make life easier for consumers. Product ranges create choice, and brands simplify this choice by providing landmarks which are strongly identified with the end-benefit sought by the consumer, a process known as brand positioning. For example, Volvo makes solid cars, while Fiat makes attractive, inexpensive cars. Loyalty makes the purchasing process even simpler. In time, it develops familiarity and confidence, like all the familiar objects around us that form an indissociable part of our everyday life. These are some of the collective – generic and structural – functions of brands. What we need to ask is whether it is now enough, or even necessary, for brands to be reassuring.

Risk and desire

One of the most significant social developments in the last 20 years has taken place in the sports sector. The list of popular sports, which had remained unchanged for almost a century, was suddenly extended by a proliferation of new sports, each more dangerous than the last: surfing, roller-skating, off-piste snowboarding, free-falling, 'bagging' mountain peaks. The common factor shared by all these sports, apart from their individual nature (they are no longer collective sports), is the desire for speed, for experiences in extreme conditions, to push back the limits. It is as if risk, far from being something to be avoided, in fact forms the very basis of the desire and excitement. Of course, not all sportsmen and women practise these sports, but they have considerable appeal to young people. For them, there is no element of risk, they simply don't see it in these terms. They are looking for excitement rather than reassurance.

Shouldn't the same rationale be applied to brands? Behind each particular brand there is a vision of what is legitimate or not to do, to think, to enjoy. We should be careful not to confuse the function of brands in general with the function of a particular brand within its own market. Especially in mature markets, where most of the brands in contention are quality brands, is it in fact desirable for a particular brand to be perceived only as reassuring? Hasn't this become an almost generic brand function, which is necessary but not alone sufficient to ensure the survival of the brand? In societies where material needs are by and large satisfied, growth cannot occur without the stimulation of desire. *The function of brands therefore becomes one of encouraging consumers to take risks:*

- by trying new technologies – digital interactive televisions and stereo equipment, biological washing powders and cosmetics;
- by trying new foods and developing new eating patterns;
- by trying new fashions;
- but also by paying less for what they buy in sectors where price has traditionally been directly proportional to quality. This is the mission of brands such as Nivea, Bic, Dop, Dim, Moulinex, and distributors such as Carrefour, Tesco and Gap.

Distributors' and manufacturers' brands

When it comes to distributors' brands, the store brand is the most typical. It combines three values: place, product and bond.

One of the key functions of store brands is to put the distributor's name on the widest range of products possible. It provides a transverse response to consumer demand, whereas the industrial sector is organized in vertical specialization. Even the Nestlé brand, which displays its name on products from powdered milk to mineral water, does not have the same transverse scope as the Swiss grocery retailer Migros or Carrefour. The customers who wheel their trolleys from one shelf to the next also have 'transverse' expectations: health, safety, shape, practicality, the simplification of their everyday life. The presence of a broadband transverse brand therefore has the benefit of clarifying the offering and providing a practical landmark for customers who want to simplify the choice process.

Through the confidence that they manage to instil over time, store brands also encourage customers to 'de-programme' themselves and explore lower price brackets. In this respect, they can make product families and markets more accessible. Not all store brands have the necessary status to do this, but some have achieved it through reliability and sheer determination. For example, the sports superstore Décathlon appeals to the desire, so far blocked by price, to participate in sport or in a lifestyle that is perceived as athletic. Décathlon brand products offer quality at low prices: unbeatable value for money.

In many product categories, confidence and the stimulus of low prices which relaxes financial constraints are the trump cards of

Table 3.1 Brand functions and the challenge from distributor's brands

Sources of Brand Added Value	Typical Product Category	Power of the Manufacturer's Brand
recognition cue	kitchen rolls	weak
ease of purchase	socks	weak
guarantee, reassurance	food	contested, average
sign of optimum performance, progress	services, cosmetics, detergents, stereos, cars	strong
emotional identification	ready-to-wear clothing, perfume	strong but challenged by vertical brands (Gap, Habitat)
permanence, familiarity	brands that inspire confidence, leading local brands	strong but challenged
enjoyment, feeling of pleasure	brands that appeal to the senses	strong
ethics and responsibility	major brands and leading companies	strong but challenged (IKEA, Body Shop)

persevering distributors. In certain product categories, the replacement of an own brand by the Carrefour brand, for example, doubles consumer demand, even vis-à-vis a recognized market leader (Lewi and Kapferer, 1998).

Functional analysis reveals how brands create value. Today, however, this value can also be created by successful distributors' brands, especially the so-called 'third type' or innovative distributors' brands. The analysis in Table 3.1 identifies the contested areas of added value, the functions in which distributors' brands are challenging the dominance of leading brands. As can be seen from the table, the first three basic brand functions are no longer enough to protect manufacturers' brands. Faced with the innovative distributors' brands that are beginning to dominate the shelves, manufacturers' brands run the risk of being relegated to the top-of-the-range 'slot' reserved for products that are not needed every day. This would seriously affect their economic survival.

If this is the case, manufacturers' brands, if they are to survive, need a shot in the arm; they should remember that we are living in the West, or at least in the affluent society. This means that we no longer have to feed ourselves, we take care of ourselves, of our bodies, our appearance and our palate. Within this context, the function of leading manufacturers' brands is to make privilege more accessible. In this way they are different from luxury brands and top-of-the-range brands. The brand must continue to remain the symbol of the affluence and progress which it simultaneously represents and makes more accessible. It is the driving force of the product category.

Over and above consumption, a simplistic – almost archaic – term if ever there was one, individuals get tangible satisfaction as well as more intangible benefits from a particular brand. Excessive store branding equalizes the market. You only have to look at the Décathlon brand, which is now represented on every sports ground in Europe, to realize the limitations of the store brand that has become too dominant.

By segmenting the markets, the brand remains an instrument of identity and prevents saturation. Hence the importance of continually strengthening the emotional bond between brands and their customers using the unique weapon of communication.

Fortunately, methods of communication have become more sophisticated thanks to the new information technology and are now interactive. But the key to brand success will always be innovation, since this is what makes brands a source of newsworthiness, desire, progress and euphoria – in short, everything which enables us to transcend the norms of everyday life. Brands must be ambitious on behalf of their customers. This has led to an increase in the speed at which new products are brought on to the market, and a decrease in the life expectancy of the products themselves. It is also the only way to avoid the boredom brought about by excessive brand loyalty. Today, Yoplait's new products have a lifespan of no more than three years. This is partly due to the fact that they are extremely popular with a small nucleus of consumers who buy a lot of Yoplait products and therefore tire of them more quickly. In addition, success stimulates distributors' copycats.

It is therefore essential to continually create and reinvent to stimulate purchasing in today's changing world of consumer loyalty.

Loyalty and innovation

The age of purely reassuring brands is over. Peugeot has finally emerged from the spiral of lethargy which threatens all purely reassuring brands with the launch of the 205 GTI, the car that created a new 'prototypical' product for the brand, especially among young and European consumers.

This decline in the value of mere reassurance is paralleled by a decrease in hereditary loyalty: 'My grandfather always bought Peugeots, my father bought Peugeots, so I buy Peugeots.' This phenomenon is becoming increasingly rare. So it's up to innovation to appeal to and win over prospective consumers. Today, consumers must be induced to feel compulsorily they 'must have' a particular new car. This is what we called the 'appropriation model' of consumer behaviour (see page 4). Hence the importance of aesthetics and daughter brands in increasing this unreasoning desire for ownership. For example, in Europe, how many consumers, who were previously uncommitted or indifferent to Renault, have been won over by the Twingo or the Scenic?

Today, in a competitive market that has eliminated all but the very best brands, only innovation can create loyalty. With each new cosmetics collection, Bourjois has to prove itself by presenting colour and product ranges that are more attractive than those of its competitors. The modern woman does not think in terms of consumer loyalty. She wants to be systematically won back by the skilful creation of innovative products and services. Loyalty is therefore the consequence of buying the brand new products, not a preliminary enduring consumer state.

Finally, it cannot be stressed enough that innovation is the natural domain of manufacturing expertise. Not subscribing to this premise is to deny the very function of the brand.

A sense of mission

In today's intensely competitive world, each brand must have a strong sense of its own mission. Without a strong raison d'être, how can it convince its employees and its consumers? Companies must regularly redefine the bases of each of their competing brands in order to eliminate weak brands or brands that have become marginalized. To do this, they must ask the following simple but essential questions about each brand:

1. What is its strong, intimate, personal vision?
2. What really creates a need for it?
3. What does it actually aim to change in the market and offer consumers?
4. What leverage or 'muscle' does it have to transform this ideal into reality?
5. What values does it offer to share with its customers, over and above the basic functions and attributes of its products?

Energy is generated when in-house teams are totally committed to the mission: they know why they exist and all individual doubts have disappeared. In continental Europe, McDonald's faces the local competitor Quick. Until Quick's franchisees understood its mission, they continued to wonder why they weren't part of the McDonald's fast-food chain.

Nothing is more communicative than the energy and strength of conviction born of a mission that is well understood and adhered to by in-house teams. This is particularly true in the case of challenger brands. Their task is particularly difficult because they have to challenge the status quo, an objective that takes audacity, in terms both of ambition and of communication style. They have to break into the market and impose their own view. Virgin does that very well.

Today, this sense of mission must be continually borne in mind and redefined, even by the leading brands since they have either become the challenger brands, vis-à-vis distributors' brands, or have a vested interest in perceiving themselves as such and recruiting managers who like a challenge. With the increasing power of consumers and distributors, it will take more to survive than simply offering reassurance. Not to mention the fact that challenger brands are always going to challenge, if not their market share, but their newsworthiness, thrill and excitement.

Leader and challenger brands

Without courage and even a touch of madness, challenger brands simply wouldn't exist. Since they start out with considerably fewer resources, in markets where the leader brand represents the status quo in purchasing terms, it takes courage, commitment and exceptional motivation on the part of their staff. It also takes courage on the part of the consumer not to buy the obvious choice, the market leader, to which a large part of the display is devoted. It should be remembered that the leader brand defines the very ideal attributes of the product category, which is obvious when you remember it was responsible for creating it in the first place (one of the facets of the so-called pioneer effect). Thus, the ideal hamburger for most consumers is a Big Mac. What do they expect from a Cola? Nothing, since Coke dominates the category and therefore defines our expectations. Is it possible to be more obvious than the leader which has utterly simplified not only the consumer's, but also the distributor's task? Of course not.

This is why *challenger brands have no alternative but to contest the single line of thought, to take consumers by surprise by challenging the status quo*:

- By creating their own market in which they themselves become the referent. In the United States, it took courage to challenge Smirnoff, the leader in the vodka market, by developing a super-premium segment that was 30 per cent more expensive. However, this is exactly what Finlandia followed by Absolut did, two brands from countries that were not traditionally associated with vodka in the eyes of American consumers (Morgan, 1998).
- By arousing curiosity and desire through the expression of a strong personality or identity, as in the case of Apple's challenge to IBM. It was also the approach adopted by Virgin Cola or Pulp, boosted by the provocative image associated with the Virgin brand, and which now has greater appeal for young Europeans than Pepsi-Cola. In its time, Pepsi also provided a good illustration of the process when it challenged Coca-Cola in a bid to differentiate itself in terms of personality (younger consumers) rather than product. Unfortunately, its success was compromised in Europe where it was too often used as a promotional or special offer brand by multiple retailers.
- By overtaking the leader in a central aspect of the brand category. This happened in the case of Burger King, whose very name indicates that it doesn't suffer from an inferiority complex vis-à-vis McDonald's, while its leading product (the Whopper) is a truly gastronomic hamburger that makes the Big Mac pale into insignificance. It was also what Schneider Electric – the world's only major electrical and integrated services specialist – tried to do in the industrial sector by competing with the international leaders in the field of general electrics: Abb, General Electric and Siemens.

General and specialist brands

An examination of the structure of the Danone brand (Kapferer and Laurent, 1998) reveals that its central nucleus consists of two products: Danette and natural yogurt. The brand has in fact created two very different prototypes. Danette's cream desserts evoke pleasure, indulgence, an absence of restraint and constraints (sugar, cream, high-fat content). All these images are absent from the natural yogurt which is pervaded by an almost Zen-like image of health and purity.

The basic mission of the leading general brands is to reconcile opposites, to make it possible for alternative lifestyles to coexist within their brand range. The leading brand names are universal, all-encompassing, generous and tolerant. Danette adds a touch of humanity to plain yogurt, while the latter prevents the consumption of Danette from being perceived as intrinsically 'bad'. It is their coexistence that creates meaning and is the mission of the brand.

In this respect, the leading general brands are different from specialist brands which have clearly stated their allegiance. Chambourcy, which used to represent pure indulgence, certainly had its attraction but also its limitations in terms of umbrella branding and therefore growth. Similarly, Weight Watchers, Bjorg, have chosen to be 'narrower' brands specializing in pure, austere health.

If specialist brands or new brands are guided by a coherence principle, generalist brands should realize that coherence becomes too often uniformity, and creates monotony. Generalist brands have more degrees of freedom: they promote peaceful coexistence.

four

The product and the brand, revisited

Today, 'value' is the key word in all discussions on branding, with companies proclaiming and defending their values: Virgin, Body Shop, Nike, Orange, Amazon to name but a few. This obsession with values leads companies to look increasingly to the realm of the intangible for a brand's raison d'être. This trend has several origins:

- Value is designed to be a response to the rationalist dialogue of distributors' brands which are based on value for money. Distributors' brands offer an exchange, while leading brands offer a gift, something extra: they offer to share their aspirational values with the consumer, over and above the basic functions of the product. By enveloping themselves in aspirational values they create a link with their target, an emotional bond that is not reduced to the issue of ingredients. This is the basic difference between the yogurt drinks Yop and Dan'up. Yop symbolizes freedom while Dan'up symbolizes nothing at all but yogurt to drink.
- The dialogue on the original (ie founding) value of the brand plays on the association with 'added value' and value creation, key concepts in modern strategic analysis.

The consequence of this emphasis on values is that marketing teams, encouraged by advertising agencies, are tending to abandon any form of dialogue on the rational justifications for consuming their particular brand. For example, advertising for Yop only conjures up images of fun, freedom, a particular lifestyle and even verges on the provocative and suggestive. Yop only presents the intangible aspects of its identity. Is this healthy? Doesn't it weaken a brand to sever all links with its more rational aspect, in this case healthy indulgence, especially with regard to the new consumer segments coming on to the market?

Basically, the gradual abandonment of the rational aspect of brand identity by managers is related to the life cycle of the brand.

The life cycle of the brand

As illustrated by Figure 4.1, brands do not originate as brands, but as a new product or service whose characteristics are different from those of its competitors and are designed to meet the needs of their target group(s). To become a brand, it must first of all prove itself as a new product. When the Nike brand was first created, Phil Knight did not talk of values and personal bests when he met buyers from the distribution sector, but of the exceptional quality of his sports shoes and their equally exceptional arch support. Similarly when consumers are asked about Nike, they don't immediately mention the United States or the ideal of individual success, but shoes with a particular quality or qualities which make them unique and desirable. For consumers, existence precedes essence: this is true both historically (their initial contact with the product is on a display stand alongside other products) and psychologically. When describing brands, consumers move from the concrete to the abstract, from the tangible to the intangible, from the product to the image, from the means to the ends. Over time, and with the accumulation of advertising images and the sponsorship of the personalities carefully chosen by Nike, the brand has acquired an additional significance which makes it not only unique and superior but also special, ie unsubstitutable, irreplaceable. It is the emotional aspect of the brand that contributes to this special character.

Initially, then, the product carries the brand. The brand is an outcome of an innovation. Over time and as products are reinvented, upgraded (competition will out!), the brand tries to monopolize the constituent values of its category by shaping them to its

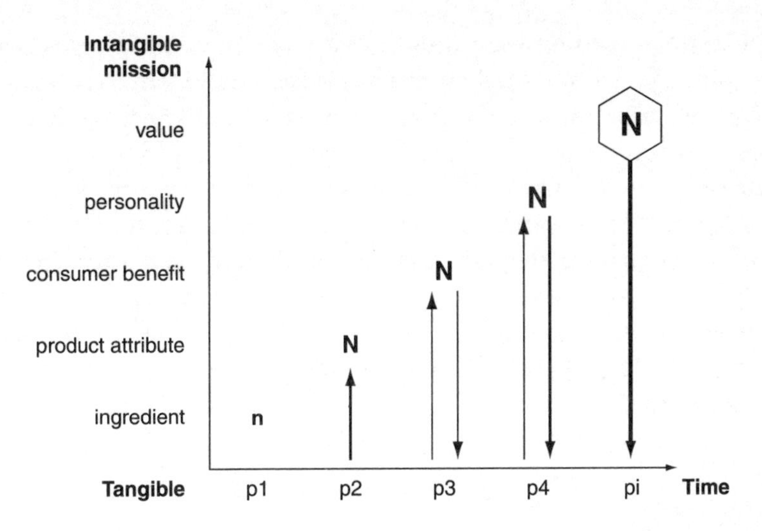

Figure 4.1 The life cycle of the brand: from the tangible to the intangible

own image. Yop made its yogurt drink a symbol of audacity and freedom, while Dan'up remained a yogurt drink.

This is why, during the life cycle of a brand, the relationship between the brand and its products is reversed. The identity of the brand is enhanced by various facets, above and beyond the purely physical aspect: its personality; its inspirational values; the image of the typical consumer. The mistake is to believe that this enhancement means substitution, but this is why marketing teams tend to concentrate almost exclusively on the intangible values. For example, Petit Filou, a fromage frais by Yoplait, was originally positioned as a 'good for growing bodies' brand. Today adverts for Petit Filou focus entirely on 'growing up happy'. Exit the calcium-growth connection. This tangible, material attribute has been pushed out. It should be reinstated and restated. Its competitor, Gervais, makes – and states – the connection, which puts Petit Filou at a disadvantage by discrediting it, as evidenced by the surveys carried out on brand image. Much more seriously, it ignores new mothers.

In fact, in all markets, beyond the specific case of our example, aimed at mothers and young children, the target group is continually renewed. By focusing on the intangible values, companies tend to forget the need to keep going back to the beginning in order to appeal to new mothers, who have to be repeatedly won over. The life cycle of the brand must be reconstructed for each new target group which doesn't know that Petit Filou is a growth concentrate.

Similarly, to return to the example of Yop, the absence of a rational basis can weaken the brand in respect of brand stretching. It limits Yop to a single provocative gesture: a liquid drunk from a bottle. In terms of this image, a solid Yop would simply not be Yop. The same applies to another Yoplait product, Zap, a yogurt drink in a sachet. After making the point in its advertisements that it seems strange to eat without a spoon, what else is there to say? What is the long-term justification for eating Zap? To conclude, the tangible should never be replaced by the intangible, as is so often the case, but enhanced by it.

Brand identity revisited

The above examples demonstrate that, although brand managers may focus exclusively on the intangible aspect – the values and abstract concept – of brands, consumers often define brand identity in terms of very concrete, palpable and tangible attributes.

For example, would Perrier still be Perrier without its large bubbles and distinctively shaped bottle? Nestlé would like to reduce the strength of the bubbles since this would make it easier to drink two or three glasses one after another and thereby create the potential for increased volume which has currently reached its limit. But wouldn't changing the bubbles mean changing the brand identity? Vache-Qui-Rit (Laughing Cow) cheeses conjure up the image of a soft-textured cheese. It would be impossible to imagine a solid Vache-Qui-Rit.

It is important to remember that the basic elements of brand identity and consumer choice are partly physical, ie tangible.

Even consumers buying a Porsche to prove they are successful need to rationalize their choice in physical terms: speed, power, road-holding ability, engine sound, a particular 'look'... In fact, when Porsche began selling cars that didn't have the traditional 'packaging' of the 911, or the engine at the rear, or the characteristic engine sound of the 911, consumers declared that this wasn't a proper Porsche. So how do you identify the attributes that constitute a brand's basic identity, its invariable central core? Surveys carried out on brand image don't offer much of a clue. It is a mistake to believe that the most widely attributed characteristics are necessarily part of this identity.

To find out whether an attribute is or isn't part of the brand identity, you have to ask consumers if the brand remains intact without that particular attribute. Is Perrier with small, light bubbles still a Perrier? Is a motorcycle without the characteristic engine sound still a Harley-Davidson? This approach was developed in 1948 by Salomon Asch, a psychologist working on social perceptions and the formation of images. Inspired by Gestalt psychology, he attempted to isolate the qualities that structure the overall perception of a person. He believed that these qualities formed the central core, while the rest were peripheral and flexible. Asch used the approach to demonstrate that the overall perception was not in fact the sum of all the qualities attributed to a particular person, but was generated by a number of 'core' qualities. In this respect they have a genetic function.

Each brand should know what are its 'core' elements but, as far as it is possible to judge, this is far from being the case. And yet the methodologies are well established. They entail asking if the brand remains the brand if it does not have an attribute, be it tangible or intangible. Those whose absence disqualifies the brand are necessary to the brand identity. They are the core.

Distributors' brands: an unwritten contract

It is a well-known fact that a brand can be compared to a tacit agreement, an implicit contract, and is in fact regarded as such by consumers. This unwritten contract, renewed with each purchase, is binding for the company in question. Companies could hardly expect consumer loyalty without commitment on their part. Brands imply duties as well as rights.

However, it is important to consider the difference between the contracts associated with manufacturers' brands, distributors' brands and generic or cut-price products, since they are all very different in nature.

The unwritten contract associated with cut-price or generic products is quantitative in nature. It is based on the concept of providing more for less: more kilos, more litres, more metres, more sardines, more slices of ham, for prices that are continually being reduced. In so doing, and as evidenced by their success, they establish an emotional bond based on the consumers' feeling of having been finally understood. Cut-price products address the consumers' dilemma of wanting to buy something they can't necessarily afford. For example, at Christmas, less-well-off consumers also want to buy *foie gras*, caviar and smoked salmon, Scotch whisky and champagne. Cut-price products try to combat the exclusion of everyday consumption, which denies access to a particular product category on the basis that certain consumers won't be able to afford it.

Cut-price products also 'understand' the logic of the consumer situation: depending on our situation, our needs fit more or less closely into a particular product category. Isn't it rather excessive to buy a top-brand orange juice, such as Tropicana, when organizing a party for 20 or so children? Doesn't it make sense to reduce the cost of the party and have more parties?

Generic products 'understand' collective logic better than any other product group: from large families through groups, organizations, canteens to small informal celebrations between friends.

The distributor's brand or store brand operates on a different level: value for money. Implicit within its contract is a process of finding suppliers (often local SMEs) with very precise terms of reference: trying to do as well as the national brand by producing good-quality but less expensive products. For example, Senoble has become France's third largest manufacturer of yogurts (behind Danone and Yoplait), specializing in distributors' yogurts and supplying their store brands. The distributor's brand represents a desire to change the structure of consumption by replacing the appeal and seduction of a wide range of brands by loyalty to a single, horizontal brand (multiple product categories). For example, Sainsbury products symbolize the wise, rational choice made by 'informed' consumers. The store brand offers a relationship based on confidence: 'I have made the right choice for you, I am therefore the right choice.' This explains why the distributor's brand has been able to extend into so many categories of products and even services. Its justification is not know-how but the service offered.

The so-called 'third type' distributors' brand – for example Reflets De France, the exclusive brand of the former Promodès group now merged into Carrefour – is more closely associated with the manufacturer's brand contract. *It targets committed consumers who are not seeking to simplify choices but improve their general standard of living.* Reflets De France operates as a collective brand for small- and medium-sized manufacturing companies which could not sustain a brand on their own but which have the joint potential to meet the demand for its products. It required the intervention of a distributor to guarantee access to super- and hypermarket shelves (which would otherwise be virtually impossible for SMEs) and, above all, to bring together over 100 SMEs under a single umbrella and single set of specifications.

The manufacturer's brand contract is particularly special. Because a strong brand not only has a successful product and service but also a brand set of evocations and symbolic meanings, consumers buy the symbol as well as the product. We consume all facets of its identity:

- the physical aspect of the brand, ie its product, performance and associated services;
- its personality, which may or may not be represented by a brand icon which boosts its symbolic potential;
- its values (drinking Virgin is more than just drinking a cola);
- the implicit relation (eg Virgin is associated with freedom).

Finally, we construct our own identity via the last two facets of the prism of brand identity: consumer reflection (vis-à-vis the outside world) and self-image (which validates our own concept of self).

Brand identity increases the strength of the bond and gives it emotional depth. It doesn't excuse weakness on the part of the product itself, but tends to make the brand less replaceable. A strong brand should be unique, superior and special (Zyman, 1999). It is the brand identity that provides this 'special' quality. This is why Yop has become a youth cult brand in France, with 86 per cent of the market share.

It is also why, in competing with distributors' brands, manufacturers' brands must not allow themselves to be drawn into making simple product comparisons. Accepting these comparisons means accepting the reduction of the brand to the status of a mere product, to its purely functional attributes. Although brands should continually be looking for an advantage with regard to this particular aspect of their product(s), they should not, however, be reduced to this advantage. There will be no shortage of competitors willing to do just that, or comparative tables in the press or on Web sites or 'shopbots'. Symbolism can't be listed in comparative tables: it is part of a brand's 'irreplaceability'.

It is therefore vital to create a strong identity that covers all facets of the brand, which is why so many pharmaceutical products are not brands. For laboratories, all products are reduced to their constituents. The creation of any form of added value which, far from replacing the superiority of the product, would give it a stronger identity and increase its impact, is still rare. Some of these products have become brands almost by chance, or reluctantly, during a media crisis that runs out of control. This is what happened in the case of Prozac, which the press made the symbol of our new society: permanent happiness thanks to a wonder pill.

Transparency and opacity

Given the nature of its unwritten contract, the manufacturer's brand has to find a happy medium between transparency and opacity in its communication. It is not by chance that major brands keep their recipes secret at all costs (eg Coca-Cola), while others have deliberately complicated it to avoid being reduced to a simple formula (12 per cent pulp in the case of Orangina). Generally speaking, each time a product becomes 'transparent', the brand is weakened. Here, transparency means that the marks of quality become accessible to the consumer, which reduces the sphere of the brand's perceived 'irreplaceability'.

This is what differentiates the fruit juice market – where manufacturers' brands are weak compared with distributors' brands – from the soft drinks market where their brands are strong.

However, soft drinks are little more than water, sugar, bubbles and vegetable extracts. The difference lies in their opacity: soft drinks are completely 'opaque'. What exactly is Sprite? How do you reduce it to a formula or a product? Quite simply, you can't. By contrast, Pampryl is freshly squeezed – Floridean, Moroccan or Israeli – orange juice, with a concentrate base, in a PET bottle. Since none of these attributes is an exclusive property of Pampryl, its quality is totally objectivized and can therefore be imitated. If the distributor Carrefour decided to bring out an equivalent, Pampryl would have little or no added value compared with the Carrefour product in the eyes of the consumer. The same cannot be said of Coca-Cola and Carrefour Cola.

The practical difficulty is that, while too much transparency is harmful, excessive opacity sometimes makes consumers wary. During the French relaunch of its infusions category (which had previously targeted the old and the ill), Unilever created the brand Saveurs Du Soir based on the concept of the modern appeal of a new product made from a subtle blend of flavours. Over time, and given their increasing sensitivity with regard to the food sector, consumers began to feel ill at ease with the lack of definition of the products used in Saveurs Du Soir (eg 'infusion from the Indian subcontinent'). The product definition therefore had to be made more transparent, which meant reducing the part played by alchemy, in order to bring the brand into line with such competitors as Lipton, whose simple infusions are made from well-known ingredients (red berries).

The balance between opacity and transparency is achieved on a day-to-day basis by constantly making readjustments. Sometimes whole product categories become overly transparent, which happened in Europe in the case of bicycles. Although most people can give examples of brands in this category – Peugeot, Raleigh, Gitane, Bianchi – these are now in the minority and have been overtaken by Décathlon, Go Sport, Nakamura (Intersport) and Micmo (the hypermarket brand). Now all these distributor brands have switch gears made by Shimano and advertise the fact in their promotional advertising and on their products. Since this major mark of quality is both transparent and common to all brands, it is understandable that price became the main criteria. Only the US brand Cannondale has protected its identity by rejecting any form of co-branding and allowing only its own brand name to appear on its bicycles. Apple has done the same whereas most other brands of microcomputers advertise the quality of their Intel microprocessor, which is common to all and therefore cancels out part of the brand differentiation. Hence it is easy for Carrefour to have its PCs made from well-known brand components such as Intel, and to claim parity with well-known PCs.

five

To brand or not to brand?

We should not allow ourselves to be blinded by the interest in branding. Even if, in modern parlance, the word 'brand' seems to have the edge on all other terms and facets of marketing, we should not allow ourselves to be hypnotized by it. Today, everybody wants a brand, as if it were the panacea of modern management. It seems to be a case of 'brand or bust'. Isn't this rather excessive?

Branding does not replace marketing

Brands are not limited to mass distribution and are systematically conquering new territories: heavy industry, the chemical industry, public services, tourism. However, the questions asked by these new sectors reveal a certain confusion, if not an illusion. For them, branding is first and foremost an act of communication: we brand therefore we are. This explains why they focus on marks, logos, names and advertising budgets. Now it should be remembered that branding in fact means associating a mark (name, etc) with an offer of value. The real question to be asked should therefore be: what added value do we want to associate with our name? Which gives rise to a stream of 'marketing' questions: for whom is it added value? What indicates that these people really value the offer? Can it be maintained in the face of our competitors? Do we have the resources to sustain its implementation? It is easy to see that the prerequisite of branding is the concept with its tangible (the product) and intangible elements. The product may already exist, in which case the function of the brand is to publicize it. But more often, this is not the case and the offer therefore has to be defined and delivered as a reality. This is a lot harder than a straightforward advertising exercise.

What return on investment?

In all competitive sectors, general managers ask coldly, and quite rightly, about the return on investment of a particular brand policy. Such policies have costs which are certain and returns which are not. The concepts of reputation, image and attitude don't count for much in this age of added value and the all-powerful shareholder. It is a fact that many of the major brands killed off by their own companies were well known prior to their demise: Treets, Philips white goods, Chambourcy, to name but a few. It is therefore necessary to prove that these psychological measures can still create value, but this time for the company. For example, to evaluate Onyx, the master brand for its waste collection and processing companies worldwide, Vivendi expects an assessment of what these indicators represent in terms of additional invitations to tender in a consultative capacity, an improvement in the success rate for these same invitations to tender, the retention of concessions and so on.

At what level should the brand be positioned?

Some companies prefer to promote their brands rather than themselves. This is why Procter & Gamble is not particularly well known by consumers, while its brands – Ariel, Tide, Dash, Pampers, Always, Mr. Clean, Pantène – are famous. In this case, the offer of value is made at product level. By contrast, information technology and high-tech products communicate at the level of the company whose credibility and expertise have turned its name into a brand. These different stances illustrate the major strategic choice that has to be made by each company, namely the optimum level at which the brand should be positioned to capture value and therefore profit.

For example, should the CLT (Luxembourg Broadcasting Company) develop the reputation of its satellite Astra, which transmits the digital images of the Canal Satellite television channel? Would this create an added value likely to influence end-users? On the contrary, isn't most of the added value in this sector now found in the services associated with such TV channels as Canal Satellite and Sky TV, which would suggest that the brands should be positioned exclusively at this level. Or perhaps it is time to create 'branded' channels like Muzzik or Eurosport? Do all the players involved in the value chain aspire to be a brand, ie invest in order to become the mark of a much-sought-after added value? Of course not. It all depends on what constitutes value in the eyes of the consumer.

So, in terms of the above example, where should the brand be positioned?

- At the level of the assembler, who gathers channels together around a particular concept?
- At channel level, for example the Disney Channel or CNN, which are indispensable to any complete multichannel package?
- At technical support level, in this instance the satellite, which makes it possible to increase the number of digital channels? Tomorrow it will provide the Internet via satellite and complete interactivity.

The question should be addressed in the light of the probable development of multichannel packages which, as in the United States, are no longer an exclusive deal. For example, the interests of the Disney Channel cannot be identified only with those of Sky TV or Canal Plus, and TPS, a newcomer, will soon have access to it.

The problem of deciding at which level to position the brand in respect of an added-value channel is a strategic one since the long-term stakes are high, as are the investments, while the returns are uncertain. Furthermore, the parameters to be taken into account are those of modern strategic analysis: the durability of the competitive advantage, the size of the market, the nature of new players, an analysis of the migration of profit associated with customer evolution (Slywotzky, 1998).

When deciding on the level it is crucial to avoid all forms of narcissism: organizations naturally like people to talk about them, but is this necessarily a source of value?

These questions concerning the level of brand positioning do not only involve service providers, but also the food industry which has recently discovered the strategic interest of 'ingredient' brands, ie at infra-product level.

The new appeal of ingredient brands

Most people have heard to a greater or lesser extent of LC1, the brand launched by Chambourcy-Nestlé in 1994 in response to the rising tide of dietetic products, especially ultra-fresh products containing bifidus. The market was created in 1986 by B'a (named after active bifidus), before being taken over to great advantage by Danone with Bio and its extensive promotional resources. In 1994, Nestlé took dietetics one step further, claiming a genuine medical benefit for a food product. The company's aim was to launch genuinely 'medically beneficial foods' with the backing of its research centre (CRN), which employs 350 researchers from 35 different countries. LC1 was the first product to claim to be a functional food. As well as improving the digestion, it also claimed to prevent illness by strengthening the body's immune system.

LC1 is in fact based on a new type of lactic ferment, different from the Bifidobacteria of B'a and Bio. It took four years to select LC1 (acidophilic lactobacillus 1) from some 3,500 cultures in the CRN's culture bank. The advertising slogan claimed that LC1 would 'help your body to protect itself'.

The results of the launch were disappointing. Numerous audits recommended changing either the brand's positioning, its packaging or the advertising campaign. In fact the problem should have been addressed at a completely different level. Should LC1 have been launched as a product brand, with its own range, or would it have been wiser to launch LC1 as an ingredient brand, ie at a lower level?

The chemical and pharmaceutical industries have become skilled in the art of ingredient brands. All the major chemical companies manufacture elasthane, the synthetic fibre that gives textiles elasticity. One company – Du Pont De Nemours – differentiated its elasthane to the point of making it an indispensable sign of quality. Without it, clothes did not appear modern, supple, elastic and fashionable and now no upmarket or fashionable textile manufacturer can do without the Lycra label. The mass-market hosiery manufacturer Dim tried not using it to avoid paying the price, which was naturally higher because of its added value. However, it was forced to 'return to the fold' since its consumers associated the Lycra label with a guarantee of quality (rather like Woolmark) and glamour.

Perhaps Nestlé should have taken the time to make LC1 what Lycra has become. This would have meant developing a strategy for the distribution of LC1 within the context of the existing brands in the portfolio, in as many categories as possible. It would also have meant making LC1 a major source of profit which could be sold to all the major agri-foods companies that wanted to buy it. The profits would have been much greater, not only in terms of Nestlé's image and the need to be recognized in medical and nutritional circles, but also in terms of the host brands and, finally, the economic equation of the system.

You only have to consider the approach adopted by Monsanto to understand the huge potential of the ingredient brand, as opposed to the traditional marketing of a range brand. Monsanto invented a synthetic sweetener which was given the scientific name aspartame, the name of the ingredient. Monsanto sold this ingredient to agri-foods companies as Nutrasweet. Although the patents for aspartame will one day enter the public domain, the value is now firmly associated with the commercial brand name Nutrasweet and therefore dissociated from the predictable fate of aspartame. Thirdly, Monsanto launched its internationally popular brand Canderel as a competitor to other sweeteners on the market. This model could have been adopted in the case of LC1 and no doubt provided much food for thought at the Nestlé research centre.

Changing levels of branding

Often, brands that have been successfully positioned at ingredient level may be tempted to change to a different strategic level and become the overall product brand. For example, the rescuers of Look, the company famous for its clipless cycling pedals, announced their intention of launching a range of bicycles under the same name. Unless it is a communication 'coup', this process is fraught with danger since it will take Look into a very different market where the competition and profit outlook are completely different.

Like Lycra and Intel, Look and Shimano have become internationally recognized marks of quality. A bicycle fitted with Shimano derailleur gears is immediately associated with quality by consumers worldwide. Shimano is the undisputed world leader in its particular niche market and most bicycle manufacturers buy Shimano gears (those who don't, buy from Campagnolo, the world's second largest manufacturer of switch gears). The distributor's brands – from Micmo and Décathlon to Wal-Mart – compete with the 'big brand names' by highlighting the co-branding of the international ingredient brands (Mavic tyres, Shimano gears, Look pedals) used on their bicycles, which are still 30 per cent cheaper than other brands.

What would be the advantage to Shimano of leaving the niche that makes it a world leader? Mavic, the leading manufacturer of competition wheels, now a subsidiary of Adidas-Salomon, got it right. The added value of the ingredient would have been lost in the global product (the bicycle) when competing with other bicycles which had the same ingredient brand but were also a great deal cheaper and carried by the more dynamic local distribution networks. In France, one bicycle in two is bought in a hypermarket, and 30 per cent in specialist superstores like Décathlon. These two distribution networks distribute their own brand, while the 'famous names' (Peugeot, Raleigh, Cannondale) compete with each other in only 20 per cent of the market. Given Décathlon's plans to expand into other European countries, it is likely that the distribution profile will even extend to places (eg the Scandinavian countries) where local distribution still represents 80 per cent of sales, taking into account the enhanced value of the service. In this context, neither Shimano or Look have really a strategic interest in relinquishing their unique position in the value chain.

In the brand life cycle, the problem of the choice of level is usually posed in the form of questions about brand stretching, although it is not recognized as such. In the case of Amora (originally a brand of mustard), the progression from mustard to vinegar and then ketchup represents a change of level. It has ceased to be a product brand and become the brand of a wider range of condiments, associated with gastronomy and linked by the theme of flavouring. In the same way, in Europe, McCain is longer associated with frozen chips, pizzas, buns or iced tea, but with a wider range of generous, simple and informal US cuisine and 'fun' meals. Today the brand covers several product categories due to the level at which it decided to operate. It was the level at which it chose to position its future competition and at which it believes it will enjoy the best competitive advantage vis-à-vis distributors and consumers. The choice of level should in fact be governed purely by this consideration.

six

The end of local brands?

Unilever's recent announcement that it intended to kill off three-quarters of its 1,400 brands over the next three to five years came as no surprise. Over the years, all companies have tended to see an increase in the number of their SKUs and products in their catalogue. There is always a good – usually local – reason for satisfying a particular distributor by launching a new product or SKU. This practice is an obvious target for modern management techniques. Distributors are now familiar with the concept of rotation and have no compunction about abolishing brands that do not meet their criteria for profitability. Surely Unilever's announcement merely confirms and anticipates this process. However, if the analysis is taken one step further, doesn't Unilever's decision herald the demise of the so-called 'multi-domestic' model of brand management which, until now, appears to have differentiated Unilever and Nestlé from their major rival Procter & Gamble?

In recent years, Procter & Gamble has pursued a policy of global branding and resolutely abolished all its weaker local brands before starting on the stronger ones. Although the latter were category leaders in a particular geographical market, they had one major flaw in the eyes of P&G: they were 'local brands'. It is a well-known fact that companies seeking to maximize return on investment can make considerable savings by the cross-border homogenization of products and brands. Generally speaking, people are unaware of the considerable costs involved in producing different formats and types of packaging for different countries, and the money saved in this area can be used to meet the increasing costs of a highly concentrated and globalized mass distribution. The global model is in stark contrast to the multi-domestic model in which, although R&D is a joint initiative, as well as product platforms, end-products and consumer benefits were adapted to meet local needs, either via a single brand (whose characteristics were optimized for the local market) or via different brands (which were well known locally). The growing demands of shareholders and the concentration of distribution forced companies to reduce costs by simplifying processes and pooling resources. In this respect, de-segmentation reduces costs, whereas optimizing brands for local markets involved the additional cost of adaptation. It is likely that the pressure of mass distribution on prices and margins, combined with pressure from shareholders, will erode the concern for maintaining local differences and intensify the globalization of products and brands. Mass retailers themselves are going global, and expect their suppliers to do so for the sake of simplification. Is this the end of local brands?

The empire fights back

In 1998, one of the most successful new products to be launched in Russia was not one of the major international brands, but a new brand of cigarette: Yava Gold. The new brand was launched by British American Tobacco, the challenger to Philip Morris for control of the world tobacco market. Although BAT could have launched one of its many international brands, it decided to launch a new local brand instead.

Even more interesting was the main line of its positioning, namely national pride expressed via the advertising theme: 'The empire fights back'. This is not so much a reference to *Star Wars* as a hymn to the pride of Mother Russia. Yava Gold offers Russian smokers a new cigarette which, although of the same quality as the international brands, does not require them to abandon their national identity in favour of a global culture. Yava Gold foreshadowed Vladimir Putin.

Danone established itself in the Czech Republic with Danone yoghurts. Then Danone biscuits were launched. The experiment was brought to a halt after a while and Danone reversed its policy and decided to make the local Opavia brand a major local brand, of European quality. In Russia, Danone biscuits have been renamed Bolshevik. But make no mistake, Russian consumers don't see the brand as a mark of a nostalgic attachment to the Soviet regime. For them, Bolshevik is simply an integral part of their history, in the same way that a consumer buying Napoleon brandy is aware of the historical connotation without having to be a confirmed Bonapartist.

What is the connection between these examples? In developing countries, consumers certainly want quality, but as individuals they also want to retain a sense of national pride and identity. They are not necessarily waiting for international brands like the 'second coming'. This little-publicized phenomenon is in stark contrast to the general, and undispute, theory of brand globalization.

Globalization or Westernization?

In early 1996, the British magazine *The Economist* painted a portrait of the China of the future: in the year 2006 the better-off Chinese would wake up in the morning, wash their hair with a Procter & Gamble shampoo, brush their teeth with Colgate and, in the case of the women, put on Revlon lipstick. When their Toyota got stuck in a traffic jam, the men would light up a Marlboro, while the women would glance at the Chinese edition of *Elle* and take their Motorola mobile phone out of their handbag to call the office. When they finally got to work, they would open a bottle of Pepsi before switching on their Compaq and working on Windows.

It is possible that the advances in high technology may only be made by the big multinationals, but does this necessarily mean that all the popular brands will also be global? The above extract implies that the products of the multinationals are of superior quality to those of their Chinese competitors, and that they also have the support of more professional marketing techniques. There are a number of comments to be made on the subject:

- What may be true of China does not apply to India, where the economy has produced equivalents for most Western mass-consumer products. These equivalents supply a vast domestic market at a price that is better suited to the local standard of living (the average annual income is US $833 and almost

700 million Indians are total non-consumers), and are often better adapted to local usage and customs (Tharoor, 1997).

- What is true of the product is not necessarily true of the brand. It is important to remember that what is referred to as a 'local brand' from a European standpoint is perceived in India as a national brand. In other words, it forms an intrinsic part of everyday life in India, has always been very much the same, and is the collective property of and forms a bond within the community. Multinational companies must certainly raise the standard of quality but this can be done via the emotional medium of the so-called local brands. In terms of the size of the market, a local Indian brand targeting 300 million potential Indian consumers, can certainly rival our European brands. Furthermore, their understanding of the psychological forces that influence consumer behaviour is infinitely superior. For example, a female consumer in Calcutta will choose Vicco Vajradanti (a toothpaste based on the Ayurvedic art of healing) rather than Colgate, Lakmé rather than Revlon lipstick and, when buying a car, will prefer the cheaper Maruti brand to Toyota.
- Many 'local' brands have an international name and are therefore not perceived as local. For example, Moulinex took over Brazil's leading 'local' brand (a market with almost 200 million consumers) of ventilators and air conditioning The brand – Mallory – is a household name in Brazil and Brazilians never stop to consider that it might not exist outside their country. The same applies in France to such brands as Hollywood Chewing Gum, Brandt, Clan Campbell and Panzani, all leaders in their respective product category, but hardly sold outside France. Conversely, many so-called global brands have been remarkably successful at integrating themselves and forming such a strong 'local' connection that each country thinks it is a national brand. Thus, in the United States Rennie is regarded as an American pharmaceutical product, in Germany as a German product and in France as a French product (it is in fact Swiss). It is only recently that Ariel's advertising has begun to state the fact that it is Europe's favourite washing powder.

To return to the scenario of the future predicted for China by *The Economist*, behind the globalization of brands lies a conviction that is intrinsically ideological: the belief that brands are responsible for bringing the progress, even the happiness, previously denied to the countries which did not have them and which therefore had to rely on local brands to satisfy their needs. By promoting these brands, not only does the world gradually become a little more homogeneous, but this homogeneity is that of Western values and products (even if the brands are Japanese or Korean). From this point of view, it is hardly surprising that the automatic assertion that globalization is the only way forward for marketing originated in the West, and especially in the United States.

Local brands under threat

Today, the globalization of brands is a priority in all the major group headquarters. For example, Procter & Gamble is pursuing a resolutely European brand strategy. It wants to develop strong Eurobrands that have the same product, the same name, the same packaging, the same positioning and use the same advertising commercials. It also wants to develop a brand portfolio for Europe to meet the principal needs of consumers, with a brand for each segment of the market. This will result in the calculated elimination or modification of any local brands that don't fit into this portfolio. 'Modification' can take the form of a new name or systematic repositioning, as happened in France in the case of Pantène, initially a shampoo for men which was redefined as an international brand for women. This logic leads one to hold out little hope for the washing powders Vizir and Bonux in France, Daz in Great Britain, or Dreft in Belgium and the Netherlands. In the body-care sector, the French subsidiary has resold the brands of soap bought recently: Roger Cavaillès, Monsavon, Biactol and the famous Pétrole Hahn, which are all profitable niche brands.

This is not an attempt to question the interest of globalization. As has already been discussed, international brand expansion is justified by the scope of modern competition and the globalization of retailers themselves. Also, since the same needs are tending to emerge on all continents, they have to be met in the same way. Furthermore, the homogenization of these responses creates value since it enables costs to be considerably reduced (one factory, one marketing team, one television advertisement) and access to new opportunities, such as sponsoring international events which are seen by viewers throughout the world (the Olympic Games, the World Cup, Formula One racing, international tennis and rugby tournaments).

Encouraged by the globalization of distribution, multinationals are jettisoning local brands in order to concentrate on the apparently much more worthwhile global brands. It would be a mistake to conclude from this that local brands are no longer of any interest. The only lesson to be gleaned from these example is that P&G-type multinationals have opted for an exclusively global strategy and, possibly, that they are no longer suited to the management of strong local brands.

It is true that, at international meetings, the brand managers responsible for the status of a local brand cut a sorry figure. They appear to have been punished, nobody has heard of their local, almost exotic brand, the legacy of a past age, with a modest challenge necessarily limited in scope. By contrast, the other brand managers compare their European or international experiences with regard to those heroes that know no boundaries: the global brands.

This would appear to support the prediction made in 1983 by T Levitt, an American academic from Harvard University, that there was no hope for companies other than international brands. In fact, the annual financial hit parade of brand values only features global brands (Coca-Cola, Sony, Dell, Intel, Compaq, Microsoft, IBM, Marlboro), and many multinationals are today under great pressure to 'deactivate' local brands. Why maintain the exclusively French brand Éléphant in the tea segment when Unilever has an international brand in the form of Lipton and another called Secret Garden? Why maintain Bonux in France in the P&G brand detergent portfolio? Why maintain Dreft, even though it is the third most popular brand of washing powder in Belgium and the Netherlands, as well as being extremely profitable, the leading product in its segment with record levels of market penetration and a reputation based on 40 years of continuous advertising?

For all that, aren't local brands still of interest? Leaving aside the clichés, aren't there pockets of profitability in certain local brands? The answer is, yes.

It is not purely by chance that in India the Coca-Cola Company has taken over and developed the local No. 1 cola, Thumbs Up. The profitability of the Benckiser company, which has just merged with Reckitt & Colman, is linked to its 'niche brand' strategy which includes such geographical niches as France's Saint-Marc heavy-duty hand washing powder. Henkel has carefully preserved and developed its Le Chat (ie the cat) washing powder by positioning it as an eco-friendly brand.

It is one thing to say that some major multinationals either do not know how or do not want to manage local brands because they no longer conform to the overall strategy, culture or organization, and therefore jettison them. But it is quite another to say that local brands are of no further interest. Some local brands are a great source of value, whether or not they are perceived as local by the consumer. Furthermore, the product leaders in many categories are local, or even regional brands: for example, the beer, fruit juice and even the whisky markets in France. Retailers know it too.

The value of local brands

As market leaders, local brands are a source of value that must be energetically maintained and promoted.

- *One of the major strengths of a local brand is the deep-rooted and powerful bond forged with local consumers*. People buy a particular product because their parents bought it. The mainspring of the relationship is confidence and loyalty created by attachment. For example, in the paint sector, the ICI group is resolutely developing the international Dulux brand. We know the professionals find it advantageous to buy international brands (a guarantee of quality), but this is less true for consumers who paint their windows or shutters once every five years. This is why, in France, ICI is reluctant to discontinue the local brand Valentine even though local DIY superstores such as Castorama and Leroy Merlin are moving into the European market and are tending to prefer global brands. But to date French consumers do not see the advantage of buying Dulux which as far as they are concerned is a new brand, with no background or point of reference, ie without the reassurance implicit in the name Valentine.

Similarly, the European leader in the bicycle sector is the Swedish group Cycleurope. Its strategy is to take over all the local leaders: DBS in Norway, Monark-Crescent in Sweden, Kildamoës in Denmark, Bianchi in Italy, Gitane and Peugeot Cycles in France. None of these brands will mean anything to readers, apart from their own national brand, but DBS accounts for 30 per cent of the Norwegian market, Crescent for 20 per cent of the Swedish market and Kildamoës for 15 per cent of the Danish market. To maintain their value, these high-profile national brands have been introduced without delay into the new segments opened up by international brands (eg mountain bikes). In this way, they will retain their relevance as well as their local status.

- *The second strength of local brands, especially in developing countries, is the fact that they are adapted to the economic standards of their own particular country*. In India, a car costing US $20,000 (the price of a Ford Escort) is a luxury. A Maruti costs US $10,000 and is now backed by the know-how of Suzuki. The local cola Thumbs Up is the market leader since it is more affordable than Coke. Indian consumers are not obsessed by Western ideals: they are sensitive to price and values and have a strong sense of their own culture. The newly opened McDonald's in Bombay should not mislead consumer analysts.
- *The third strength is cultural*. The local brand creates a powerful social bond, as in the case of Ricard or Miko ice cream in France, and Oxo or Wall's in Great Britain. In France, Nestlé has a well-established local brand Ricoré (a coffee substitute), whose 250-gram container is the multinational's only product, apart from Kub Maggi, to pride itself on a 100 per cent weighted distribution (source: AC Nielsen). Some local brands are based on powerful collective local symbols, for example Saint-Marc washing powder and Javel La Croix bleach, which create a loyalty that

is simply developed by raising the quality of the products to modern standards.

- *The fourth strength of well-established local brands is their profitability*. Ricoré is probably one of the best cash cows in Nestlé's portfolio. It has a record number of loyal buyers who are attached to the brand, hooked on its taste, and resistant to change. Given the minimal investment in advertising needed to maintain this brand, it is easy to imagine how profitable it is.

It is easy to understand why many multinationals are on the lookout for good local brands with the above attributes. They make a wonderful open sesame for (distribution) doors when penetrating new markets. This is what happened when Moulinex took over Mallory in Brazil, and when Pernod-Ricard took over Larios gin in Spain: the ultimate leader in its segment with more than 60 per cent market share, and a national symbol. These extremely profitable leading brands provide an invaluable springboard for creating a portfolio of new brands, including the global ones.

A revitalization is essential

The strength of local brands lies, as we have seen, in two main factors: historical familiarity and the fact that they are much more concerned with satisfying local purchasing trends, ie of the consumers in their market. This explains some truly astonishing market shares:

- *In Switzerland,* ENKA washing powder, launched in 1908, accounts for 50 per cent of the market for pre-wash additives. Subsequent launches of all the major washing powders have never affected its market share.
- *In Norway,* Krystal, a household cleaner launched in 1916, is more popular than the global brand Ajax. Although Krystal is no more efficient than Ajax, it is a natural product made from vegetable oil, has a pleasant smell and creates good feelings among Norwegian consumers who find the brand reassuring.
- *In the Netherlands,* the No. 1 shampoo is not Pantène, Elsève or

Organics, but Andrelon, named after a famous Dutch hairdresser. Unlike the international shampoos, whose advertisements show top models straight off the catwalk, Andrelon presents 'the girl next door' and simply promises to reveal her natural beauty. Dutch women find international shampoos too thick and too 'conditioning'. The success of Andrelon lies in the fact that it takes account of the preferences of Dutch consumers.

It is tempting for companies whose main priority is marketing their global brands to 'milk' the cash cows represented by local brands. After all, bonds based on familiarity and tradition have a certain durability and ageing consumers remain loyal to their brands. This is why ENKA does not advertise. However, the company is confusing established brands with outmoded brands. The social bond is an intergenerational phenomenon. Revitalizing these brands can have an amazing effect on the younger sections of society provided, like any other brand, they are given an exciting image that makes an impact. This involves several stages:

- *Updating the design and logo,* taking great care to preserve the familiar features and even reinforce the values of the brand, for example by increasing the size of Krystal's swan logo. It is, however, important to treat the traditional product with great care, since it fulfils the function of a prototype for the brand. When Procter & Gamble took over Pétrole Hahn (a fortifying hair lotion which it has recently resold), it was careful not to change the packaging of the standard product too much, but concentrated on brand extensions and new formats.
- *Developing new formats for the product* which convey modernity and an understanding of the new types of usage required by local consumers. Krystal waited until 1972 to bring out a liquid version alongside the old cream launched in 1916.
- *Having no compunction about penetrating new markets.* DBS, the leader of the Norwegian bicycle market, began to sell mountain bikes when it had previously been classified as a producer of family bicycles. Although some young Norwegians prefer an American Cannondale mountain bike, most of the mountain bikes sold in Norway are now DBS bikes, a mark of the brand's power and latent potential. All it needed was to convert this

potential into reality and that is exactly what DBS did. This also had the effect of modernizing the brand image and increasing its market power.

- *modernizing communication while respecting values.* Krystal's advertising is now associated with WWF, the World Wide Fund for Nature.

seven

The age of efficiency

Brand management has entered the age of efficiency. Contrary to what the marketing manuals would have us believe, consumers are no longer the be-all and end-all of brand management. They have been rejoined by shareholders who, especially if their pension fund is at stake, want a good, guaranteed return on their investment. Retirement in the year 2000 must be comfortable and secure, so 'pensioners' must be assured of increasing returns on their original investment. In terms of brand management, it is no longer enough to get results and be effective, you also have to be efficient. Return on investment, previously relatively low on the marketing list of priorities, is today a top priority. In recent years, advertising costs (eg the cost of commercials) have continued to soar in all market sectors. However, there is still no tangible proof of the return on the sums invested in these mass-marketing campaigns. This is why advertising is one of the traditional practices of brand management that are currently being called into question. It is interesting that Procter & Gamble recently announced its intention to pay its advertising agencies on the basis of their results.

Facts, just facts

In theory, it should be possible to predict the return expected on each marketing investment, even if it means revising the figures as the prediction gradually becomes a reality. Whether it involves changing the logo, the brand icon or the packaging, or launching a brand extension or a promotion, today no recommendation should be made without specifying the expected financial return on the investment. Otherwise, how do you justify allocating a particular amount to one particular investment rather than another? What is standard practice for any decision concerning, say, a change in logistical methods or the construction of a new warehouse, does not, unfortunately, appear to have permeated marketing circles with the same degree of urgency. Marketing managers agree in principle but drag their feet when it comes to putting it into practice. They are still living in 'cloud cuckoo land'.

No matter how much it stresses added value, value creation and return on capital investments, marketing cannot continue to evade the efficiency issue.

As early as the 1980s, a cultural revolution took place when marketing went beyond the basic psychological measures of brand equity (reputation, image, loyalty) and introduced the financial valuation of 'goodwill' or the additional (tangible and intangible) value associated with the brand name and reputation.

For a long time, accounts were only required from the technicians involved in direct marketing and promotions. They were perceived as the only people who had the behavioural information that made it possible to calculate a return. Furthermore, evaluations of promotions were often fairly crude since they were limited to 'before and after' comparisons. Now, not only is it important to make a comparison with what would have been sold (in all probability) without the promotion, but above all to include the hidden costs of the promotion, an item that is systematically underestimated. For example, there is a general tendency to omit the costs of complexity, eg the increase in the number of SKUs for a limited period, problems of logistics and production, additional stock, time spent and so on.

Today, general managers of the major groups want to apply factual logic to all requests for marketing investments. The aim of marketing is to maximize not sales but profits. Money is scarce, so why allocate it to one area rather than another? Why allocate it to this particular brand extension? Have all the costs been weighed (opportunity, training, complexity) and compared with the alternative solution which would be to develop the standard product to make it less 'standard'?

Brand management has hidden behind qualitative research for far too long. It is as if figures were something to be afraid of. Possibly as a result of their background or training, many brand managers don't like the idea of figures. It is no longer a question of placing quantity and quality in opposition. Companies want inventive, creative managers, but also managers who can take responsibility for the sums invested. Experience shows that change rarely comes from within, as evidenced by the current fashion for big consultancy companies to help address brand-related problems.

One cannot help noticing the growing presence of such firms as McKinsey, Accenture (previously Andersen Consulting), Gemini, Mercier, BCG, Bain, etc, in what was previously the preserve of advertising agencies and their associated consultancies. This increase is linked to a number of factors:

- *A general recognition of the strategic nature of brand-related decisions* and the need to obtain advice that is independent from any vested interest in their implementation (eg who will or will not get the advertising budget).
- *The direct contact with top management* via previous assignments relating to organization, strategic investments or activity portfolios. Today, brands have less to do with marketing managers than general management.
- *The international culture of consultancies* which enables them to send consultants anywhere in the world to deliver, in the shortest possible time, what they know how to do best, ie illustrate by examples what others have already done. This presentation of 'best practices' always interests general managers since it shows that what some people thought was impossible for their company has already been done successfully by others for some time.
- Finally, *the quantitative culture*. Through training and recruitment, consultancies have turned their attention to quantification. The basic disciplines of their consultants (economics, financial analysis, cost analysis) develop an attitude and expertise that focus on the quantification of causes and their effects. The accounts of Accenture are based on factual analysis and are the only type of account general management is interested in.

Setting a hierarchy of priorities

As well as 'having the ear' of the management, the quantitative culture also has the advantage of making the decision-making process more efficient. When working on revitalizing an old brand, for example, the first thing to do is establish why the brand is perceived as being outdated. The logical course of action for any brand manager would be to carry out relevant qualitative analyses to identify the multiple causes of the brand's decline. The problem is that qualitative analysis doesn't prioritize the causes. What are the actual causes, in order of priority, of the long-term decrease in tonnage? What is the relative influence of the increase in the relative price in relation to the decrease in popularity and an ageing clientele? As long as the problem isn't couched in these terms, it will be impossible to determine the principal cause of the effect identified. It will therefore be equally impossible to prioritize investment, ie to decide what leverage will produce the best return.

Companies have the resources to adopt a quantitative approach to brand-related decisions, but they must also actively want to do it and be prepared to revolutionize internal practices. Demonstrating the feasibility of such an approach by bringing in an external firm of consultants to work with the marketing teams, with the support of general management, is an effective way of achieving this.

If the advertising sector does not respond to this demand for proven returns, it is to be feared that the advocates of other forms of communications, essentially focused on the calculation of the return, may have the last word. They are able to provide Danone's chairman, Mr Riboud, with the figures for the return on the investment in *Danoé*, a consumer magazine sent to two million consumers, or calculate the increase in the business turnover and profit margin brought in by e-business, or CRM. Micromarketing proves its results by winning over or retaining the loyalty of carefully defined consumer target groups for a particular product or category. Far be it from us to criticize these necessary forms of targeted communications which certainly do not limit themselves to the more elusive advertising contacts. However, it should be remembered that the calculation factor counts for a great deal in this new marketing craze. There was a telling example of this in early 2000, when Procter & Gamble launched its new orange-flavoured drink, Sunny Delight. The direct marketing budget was twice that of the television commercials!

Transparency and efficiency

At present, there is a contradiction between the marketing information available and the realities of brand competition. One after another, major manufacturing companies are becoming involved in trade marketing initiatives to promote their own sales alongside those of their distributors, who also have their own brands. Manufacturers are developing marketing strategies segmented by distributors, allocating staff to each distributor, and defining each distributor as a separate market. They have a number of reasons for doing this. Because of their size, distributors have more influence than geographical regions or even countries. Also, not all distributors have the same objectives or the same strategy, and their store brands don't have the same influence vis-à-vis consumers. Hence the need for joint marketing initiatives. The most recent research carried out by IRI-Sécodip on 30 product categories, in 400 supermarkets over a 52-week period, showed that the 'privilege' of each brand varied from one distributor to the next. The term 'brand privilege' refers to the fraction of the market share that is not explained by the supply side on the supermarket shelves. There is therefore an interaction between the brand and the distributor that determines the performance of each brand.

As long as individual brand managers do not receive separate statistics for each distribution outlet, the overall management of the brand will not achieve the required level of efficiency. However, the transparency of information currently practised by a number of distributors should gradually become more widespread and lead to information being made available on a store-by-store basis. This is the price of improved efficiency, for both distributors and manufacturers. It will soon be possible to identify the proportion of, say, Danone or Nestlé products on the global till receipt, and to evaluate how this proportion is affected by a promotion for a particular leading brand.

ECR and brand management

By early 2000, there was not a single supplier in the mass-distribution market that wasn't involved in some sort of ECR (efficient consumer response) initiative with its main client-distributors. Even the fruit and vegetable and meat sectors were involved. ECR is a basic cooperation initiative between suppliers and distributors to improve the value of the products and services offered to consumers. ECR usually begins with collaboration at the level of 'back-office' systems and logistics, where the aim is to reduce all costs that do not create value for the end-consumer. The next stage, known as 'category management', involves increasing the value of the category for consumers and distributors. The ultimate aim is to retain the loyalty of the major customers of the distributor and the brand, preferably both at the same time.

This is why, in modern brand management, it is essential to develop a profile of the brand's heavy buyers. It is also necessary to compare this profile with that of the major customers of the distribution outlet. If they coincide, then there is a strong convergence of interests between the brand and the distribution outlet. If not, there is little point in promoting a brand from the portfolio with a distributor whose consumer profile is too divergent.

One of the most widely discussed aspects of category management is the actual definition of the category and the distributors' choice of supplier, who will be their major adviser for the category. Categories are not in fact defined by traditional physical products but by units of need. In the drinks category, for example, instead of using product segmentation (cola, other soft drinks, mineral waters), distributors organize products according to end-use, time of day and purpose. This type of segmentation determines the new layout of the actual shelves. Thus British supermarkets always have a section and a refrigerator devoted to breakfast, separate from the unit of need devoted to refreshment or health care, for example. Some companies have adapted their brands, but especially products and formats, in this new bid to improve their efficiency.

In fact, the most extreme consequence of category management is often multiple presence in store. For example, small bottles of chilled Coca-Cola are displayed in the refrigerated 'lunch' section, next to the chilled sandwiches. It also appears in the health foods section in the form of Diet Coke, and in the pizza section and so on. By doing this, the points of contact with the brand are increased, as is the probability of purchase via the format of differentiated products. In this way Coca-Cola reduces the consumption of natural mineral waters, particularly in France where their dominant format (a six-pack of 1- or 1½-litre bottles) relegates them to the back of the store with easier access for the fork-lift trucks used to move the heavier items. By so doing, mineral water is only found in one place.

Efficiency versus regional marketing

It would appear that country by country marketing has 'gone out of style'. Everywhere, multinationals are developing a structure based on distributors and categories, at the service of a 'purified' portfolio of exclusively global brands. However, a closer look reveals that, in the interests of efficiency, even the most committed advocates of globalization still have teams devoted to the country. In fact, the multinationals realized that it was possible to create a stronger bond with consumers by getting to know them better and adapting national resources to meet their specific needs. In different countries, a process of 'fine tuning' the non-advertising resources has enabled them to optimize their marketing strategies. For example, to launch Pringles in Italy, the local P&G teams also decided to distribute them via the so-called alternative outlets (small local shops and petrol stations) to achieve a higher profile. They also used local celebrities to make Pringles an American icon that had flown in from the United States (this would have been impossible in other countries). As a result, Pringles has become a symbolic brand in Italy.

This approach implies the implicit recognition of the fundamental importance of below the line in a successful brand launch. Underground marketing has only just begun, but it was high time that the marketing sector took account of the role played by 'word of mouth' in the distribution of new products and brands (Kapferer, 1991).

Even e-brands, as soon as they need to prove their relevance in depth, have developed country by country subsidiaries. Hasn't the prototype of them all, Amazon, created Amazon.uk, Amazon.fr, etc? If fame is built on the global market space, relevance has to be demonstrated in the every marketplace, one after the other.

eight

What fast-moving means for consumer goods

All marketing managers should take out a subscription to the US magazine *Fast Company*. The magazine's central theme is to persuade companies that greater reactivity is the key to competitiveness. The Internet plays a key role in this process, in the sense that its systematic use will create new expectations with regard to brands. A Web site is, by its very nature, a living entity: nothing on it is permanent. Material must be continually renewed and updated to encourage people to want to keep visiting it, and to avoid giving the impression that nothing new is happening in connection with or on behalf of the brand.

Even without the Net, the concept of speed must be central to all modern brand management. As a living entity, a brand must continually give out messages that reflect its energy and its fundamental ability to adapt and react in a fast-developing world.

How to move consumers?

In marketing, the term 'fast-moving consumer goods' (FMCG) is tending to replace 'mass market' goods, ie the concept of speed has replaced that of mass. If we consider the reality of the situation, the term 'mass' is in fact doubly inappropriate in view of modern market fragmentation and increased consumer sophistication. Added to this, the speed at which new products are being brought out in all sectors has increased dramatically. It is by innovating that brands remain relevant, justify their price premium and confirm their status as a point of reference. In the cosmetics and fashion markets, for example, leaving aside older consumers who religiously continue to buy the same products, consumer loyalty is a thing of the past. Consumers are won over by new products and new brands. Brands admittedly enjoy a certain 'goodwill', affection and respect, but image and buying are two different things. Consumers have to be repeatedly won over by a continually renewed offering since this is the price of relevance. What is making consumers buy Bourjois this year in the supermarkets? Brand loyalty? No, it's the fact that product range has adapted to the current climate by offering fun tattoos to its modern young clientele, plus a new range of colours for make-up and lipsticks, all under the one brand name.

Innovation is the lifeblood of a brand. It enables the brand to place the new product at the centre of its advertising. This is the only way to explain the success of Dim hosiery. Men certainly see a hymn to female beauty in each of its advertisements. But women also see the new products that are an integral part of everyday life. There is not a single Dim advert that doesn't focus on a particular product, while everything takes place in the unique atmosphere of Dim commercials.

The first thing that the new Moulinex marketing team did was to place innovation, which had been neglected in previous years, at the heart of the marketing machine. Moulinex may be popular, but on the shelves the product must be attractive, relevant and have that creative edge that makes people think: 'That's really well designed, I want it.'

The outdoor pursuits brand Lafuma also tries to break the traditional mould of biannual production by launching a lot more 'special event' products linked to current events, the sort of things that make a brand part of everyday life.

It should also be pointed out that, in certain sectors, distributors' brands are not to be outdone in the field of innovation. In Great Britain, distributors launch more new products than manufacturers. Of course, it is important to define what 'new products' means in each case: an additional variety, a brand extension or an innovation in the true sense of the term. But the message is clear. Distributors' brands that want to become brands in their own right have understood the importance of a regular supply of innovative new products. Furthermore, as they use subcontractors with no advertising or referencing costs (at least no cash outlay), it is easy for them to increase the number of new products on their shelves. The cost of failure is low and the probability reduced if their own new products are inspired by the success of the new products launched by manufacturers' brands. One more reason to be a constantly moving target.

Technology: making speed the key to success

Recent technological advances have made speed the key to success in the modern 'market space'. Technology is continually enabling new products, which were unthinkable yesterday, to become today's reality. And the terms 'yesterday' and 'today' are used literally, not as a figure of speech. The case of the mobile phone is a prime example of a product category that is continually developing new functions. At the beginning of 2000, mobile phone users could listen to their e-mails and answer using voice-mail. In the weeks that followed (tomorrow) they were able to buy direct using a telephone that was able to 'read' credit cards.

Today, all sectors are affected by technology. It makes supplier–client relations much easier, and offers the added possibility of improved service and performance and greater immediacy. In the food sector, it makes new combinations of hitherto unknown textures and tastes possible... not to mention the GM foods revolution.

The result of all these technological advances is that consumers are possibly no longer the source of ideas and motivation that they once were (Christensen, 1999). In fact, consumers have little or no imagination. They could not invent a car that did not already exist, or the Internet, or the television–telecommunications–information technology combination that is currently revolutionizing their homes. Brand management means relying on the consumer at one end of the scale and, at the other, having your finger on the pulse of science and technology and knowing how to decode the signals and transform them into ideas, concepts and new products.

The importance of technology also leads to the recognition of the fact that, apart from distributors' brands, today's main competitors are the least expected, those who enter your particular category from a completely different product category! Thus Kodak's main competitor is Hewlett Packard or the Epson laser printer. In the youth market, the main competitors of the bicycle are the skateboard, snowboard or Sony PlayStation, which explains the collapse of the global bicycle market after the boom in mountain bikes.

The end of monolithism

The speed of development is also reflected in brand signs and communications. In the early 1990s, Coca-Cola took an unprecedented step by sacking its long-standing advertising agency McCann and replacing it with the more imaginative and, above all, multiple imagery of a creative 'hot shop'. This was the end of the one and only long-running commercial. To stimulate sales the brand has to be exciting. It can only be exciting by renewing its images.

This was not without consequences for its graphic identity. An examination of present practices reveals that brands are tending to abandon their monolithic identity in favour of a series of different identities. Although these are related, they are not 'cloned' and do not simply reproduce the same characteristics. Let's take another look at Coca-Cola. This is a brand with two names: Coke to represent modernity and Coca-Cola to reflect authenticity and tradition. The single, characteristic colour – red – that was used for such a long time has been replaced by a range of colours depending on the version, products and consumer benefits. Today, the Coca-Cola range is more open, more welcoming.

Everywhere, major design studios are breaking the previously sacrosanct rules of the monolithic brand identity. Brands now have different versions for their logos, symbols and the way in which they are used. Imagine a Web site that repeated the same brand logo for all targets, pages and uses. It is significant that Nestlé now uses different logos for different need categories. In the ultra-fresh food sector it uses the former Chambourcy logo. It uses another for chocolate, and another for cereals and so on. Even Nivea and Vichy vary their brand logo according to sector. You don't advertise Vichy in the same way on a sunblock cream as you do on a moisturizer.

Variety is the spice of life, and achieving it before the competition is what keeps a leading product ahead.

The brand as a living system

The rules governing the exact repetition of the same symbol are also being broken on a visual level. What counts is the overall coherence of what can be referred to as the 'brand system' (Sicard, 1998). Variety does not necessarily mean incoherence. Today, a general understanding and a convergence of style are considered more important than its mere repetition. The important thing is that the brand generates coherent images that create a common background theme. Brands such as Calvin Klein foreshadowed this trend.

In terms of repetition, what does the torrid image of Obsession actually have in common with the idealized image of Eternity? The answer is Calvin Klein, which cannot be defined as either torrid or idealized but which knows how to change with the times. The link between these very dissimilar images is the brand. Calvin Klein's spectacular presentation of a wide range of interpersonal emotions increases the brand's access to different markets. For Allure, Chanel uses a number of different top models to the same effect.

McDonald's also has developed a 'brand system', with access to several markets, from Ronald McDonald through 'Big Mac' to 'Double Arch'.

Speed and globalization

One of the effects of the globalization of the distribution sector is the speed with which new products are brought on to the market. Today, a global company in the 'fast-moving consumer goods' sector makes 25 per cent of its turnover with 20 clients worldwide. Tomorrow it will be 35 per cent. In the wake of such clients it is possible to imagine international launches that are much faster than today's approach via countries and geographical regions. This is all the more likely since certain categories of product are, in fact, ideally suited to direct marketing. Even today, there are many new product launches where, contrary to accepted practice, the investments in direct marketing (eg using mega-databases and geographical types) are greater than the advertising budget.

nine

The Internet challenges

Brands were among the first things to be affected by the Internet. One after another, they realized the importance of the phenomenon and its extremely strategic nature, in the sense that it could threaten their future if they did not react swiftly and appropriately. After all, brands owed their development to self-service stores, but it is the hypermarkets that are now eliminating them. The same could well be true of the Internet. This unprecedented distribution channel, means of communication and forum for exchange not only offers some truly fantastic opportunities, but also presents some serious challenges for brands.

The virtual megastore

All brands dream of controlling their distribution network. The deregulation of European markets has further restricted the areas in which this is possible. Even the car industry will have to adapt to a world 'without concessions', ie without exclusive dealers (Kniebihler and Giaoui, 1998). A Web site is a virtual megastore. Each site promotes the advantages of vertical brands, in the same way as Gap and Zara, who control their image and communication in their own shops, or the 'Nike town' initiative. The Web enables each brand to have its own megastore, open 24 hours a day for 365 days a year, at local and international level. Obviously not all brands have the same prospects for increasing their annual turnover via e-commerce, and the idea might be more interesting for a producer of fine wines, *foie gras* or computers, or for a financial investment company, than for major food producers such as Danone or Nestlé. Even so, these two brands run the risk of becoming banal. How can they become more than just a product? How can they revitalize their values? The answer lies in communication, complicity and service. It should be remembered that a megastore is first and foremost a place where consumers feel comfortable, where they feel at one with the values of the brand, where communication is the order of the day. Only a few distributors have managed to make their sales outlets exciting, free and interactive areas where their customers can obtain information and exchange ideas independently of any form of sales transaction: Habitat, Virgin and Décathlon are some of them. The Internet provides the opportunity to increase the available information tenfold by abolishing the constraints of time and space.

For example, when the Lvmh group launched its subsidiary Séphora (a chain of stores dedicated to beauty, cosmetics and perfumes) in the United States, it not only opened a megastore (2,000 square metres) in the heart of New York's Rockefeller Center on 14 October 1999, but also the 'cyberstore' Sephora.com to maximize the synergy between the two distribution channels.

The 'service' challenge

The consumer's relationship with a brand is not platonic. He or she expects to become physically involved and needs to be encouraged to do so. Saving consumers from having to walk or travel to a particular shop, accompanying them interactively in their choices, to the point of order and especially afterwards, is real value creation. The first form of added value on the Internet is information. But there is no point in providing information unless it enables consumers to convert their desire into an act of purchase, ie to become involved in a transaction.

Today, because this is a new phenomenon, manufacturers are caught up in conflicts over distribution channels. They don't sell direct to avoid conflict with retailers or dealers, the mass distribution sector or their own stores. This was why Levi's stopped selling direct via the Internet in November 1999. Legal considerations also come into play when a brand wants to reserve the exclusive right to sell via the Internet.

Another reason given for slowing down the creation of one vast e-commerce site is the interfaces with companies' computer systems. But these reasons cut very little ice with consumers who see this as a denial of service. When this book went to press, it was still impossible to book a holiday with Club Méditérranée via the Internet! This is somewhat surprising when you take into account that this is an international brand selling to clients worldwide, from the United States to Japan. In early 2000, few cars were being sold via the Internet in Europe, at a time when 7 per cent of new cars bought in the United States were bought online, and 40 per cent of Americans visited a manufacturer's Web site before buying a car.

In any event, the trend is irreversible and, in September 1999, Nike announced its intention to sell direct via the Internet. Distributors certainly run the risk of cannibalizing the turnover of their retail outlets – by creating problems of return for their bricks and mortar investments – if an increasing proportion of their customers stop going to hypermarkets and shopping centres but prefer to visit virtual stores in their own time. Sir Richard Branson, chairman of Virgin, summed up the inevitability of this trend for all companies, in spite of the prospect of cannibalization, when he said that even though it meant cutting off one of his own feet he preferred to do it himself.

One could say that the Internet faces a 'service challenge'. Even leaving aside e-commerce, generally speaking the Internet forces all brands to become service brands. In today's world, thanks to their high unaided awareness, brands are constantly impinging on the consciousness and choices of consumers with little or no effort on their part. In the virtual world of the Internet, brand awareness is not enough and consumers have to have good reason to visit and return to a particular site. Hence the importance of the 'use value' of the site.

This can be achieved by supplying information or advice about a product. A brand of shampoo should provide information on the latest trends in hair care and fashion, and even be able to give personalized advice. A food product should also offer serving suggestions, and clearly explained recipes illustrated by video images. This is what Unilever does in the United States for one of its brands and surveys have showed that 11 per cent of the people who consulted the site went out and bought the product to use in the recipe of their choice. The service can also provide information on activities that may be unconnected with the product but which are related in terms of the brand image. For example, a particular brand of perfume for young people could give the dates of rock concerts or sports events if these match the brand image.

There are no limits to the services that can and should be offered to consumers. The Internet is there to make life as simple as possible for them.

However, like every other form of media, the Internet has its rules. Traditional brand marketing is based on the systematic interruption of the consumer's everyday life by TV ads designed for the general market or at least wide segments. The Internet completely reverses this principle. Consumers decide to access a particular Web site and expect progressive information that is regularly updated and tailored to their needs. They do not log on to the Internet to be interrupted by advertisements. They will at most tolerate a message offering them the opportunity to double-click, thereby giving the brand permission to tell them more (Godin, 1999). This brings us to the four types of service required by Internet users.

The first service that should be offered to Internet users is to not waste their time. After all, if they are surfing the Net rather than walking around shops, it is because they are trying to maximize the use of their time. The golden rule of Internet services is that everything should be easy. However, this apparently minor expectation is continually disappointed. For example, the dialogue is too slow and the links tend to be developed for the benefit of the internal organization of the company (often fragmented) rather than the concerns of the consumer.

The second service is to recognize the difference between Internet users so as to channel them rapidly towards the level and type of information that corresponds to their specific needs. This basic requirement is, however, far from being satisfied on many sites which are more like static brochures than service sites. For example, how many of these sites record visits from users and make use of the information?

The third service is to regard the site as a store which is open 24 hours a day, not for sales but for after-sales service, which in fact forms the basis of consumer satisfaction and loyalty. It is after making a purchase that the problems really begin for consumers. Apart from hotlines (which are usually busy), it should be standard practice to anticipate all the possible problems that could occur in the use of the brand product and, via a skilfully designed system, make them accessible on the Web site so that consumers can find the solution to their particular problem. For example, the Web site of an airline company should provide continually updated information on the progress of each flight, its estimated time of arrival, the ground temperature and information on local weather conditions. The site becomes an integral part of customer service and a tool that customers can use (Seybold, 1998; Rechenmann, 1999).

The fourth service is to enable consumers to communicate freely with each other on subjects of common interest. This creates networks based on shared interests, involvement and 'word of mouth'. As a forum for the free exchange of views and opinions, the Net enables the brand to take advantage of the involvement created by these virtual communities. Although the brand must certainly create its own community, it must also recognize that community's desire for freedom. Hence the importance of these forums of common interest and values which bring consumers together around a particular brand.

The 'transparency' challenge

Taking an optimistic view of things, it is possible to advance the hypothesis that as reality becomes virtual, brands become the only points of reference, with the confidence that their name inspires, within an impalpable, intangible space. Furthermore, this hypothesis would appear to be borne out by the facts. At present, the most frequently visited sites are those of the best-known, most reputable and most popular brands. However, these tend to be brands created by and for the Web – eg Yahoo!, Amazon or Kelkoo – rather than brands in the traditionally accepted sense.

It is a recognized fact that the success of brands in the 'old economy' marketplace was partly based on the proliferation of choice, and hence the difficulty experienced by consumers when faced with the range of choice on supermarket shelves. Brands were born of the economics of incomplete and imperfect information, in which the power lies in the hands of whoever has access to the information. In the traditional economy, this information was concentrated in the hands of the manufacturers, specialist distributors, experts and prescriptors. Until recently, consumers wanting to buy a microcomputer, for example, could not reasonably expect to spend their time examining and comparing all the PCs made by every brand before making a final decision. It would have been an endless task. In this respect, it was impossible for consumers to adopt a rational approach even if they wanted to. The same principle applies to choosing an insurance policy or a skin cleanser. Brands, with their top-of-mind awareness that constantly impinges on the consumer consciousness, their accessibility, their enhanced and reassuring image, made it possible to choose more quickly and achieve a higher level of satisfaction. In fact, the aim of brand images is to make brands irreplaceable by developing the idea that they are special, inimitable and exclusive. Since consumers are unfamiliar with the alternatives, or may never even have considered them, they cannot have any regrets. Brands therefore used to capitalize on the opacity of the market and the effort involved in accessing information, which until recently was unobtainable, indigestible or incomplete.

The advent of the Internet will shift this balance of power from the brand to the consumer. It is a medium that gives easy access to information. It creates a certain transparency of offerings, prices and margins. Admittedly, at first glance, there is even more choice on the Internet. But this should lead to the emergence of new players who create transparency and bring added value. They are known as 'infomediaries' or 'shopbots' and their task is to carry out research, compare all the offerings and possibly even choose the product(s) on the basis of criteria supplied by the consumer. In so doing, these 'infomediaries' can fulfil the same function as the comparative tables published by consumer associations, which show that the major brand names are (unfortunately) not always synonymous with better quality, and suggest the products of less well-known suppliers whose performance makes them well worth a closer look. In this way, they reduce the barriers to entry in the market by promoting, if not completely unknown brands, at least less well-known brands with a lower profile image. These 'infomediaries' will therefore considerably extend the range of suppliers and brands usually consulted (three until now). Finally, they could also demonstrate that a well-known brand does not necessarily have a good performance in terms of the attributes important to the consumer and, as a result, significantly alter its image. It is obvious that this increased transparency will create an additional obligation on the part of brands in terms of their performance in the field of functional quality and objective services. They can no longer afford to rely on their reputation or enhanced image to compensate for shortcomings in these particular areas. Not all brands are Jaguar.

At the same time, the more brands are compared, analysed and reduced to objective functions, the more they must try to become incomparable and unique by developing intangible values which create the involvement that no comparative table has been able to capture. Who has ever looked at a comparative table for colas?

The 'infomediaries' will therefore either be looking for relevant information and making pre-selected choices, or making delegated choices in the light of the consumer's own specific motivations and criteria for choice. In fact, 'infomediaries' are like any other form of advice: it all depends how much confidence we have in the advisers.

Who can claim, a priori, to have sufficient credibility to be a leading 'infomediary'? Who can create a 'portal' site that will become a true forum for advice and purchasing? Specialist distributors? The professed aim of Sephora.com is to become the referent for online beauty in the United States. The absence of distributors' brands in this field currently makes Séphora an unbiased, specialist representative. Could Carrefour or Wal-Mart become 'infomediaries'? Given the desire of these two leading companies to impose their distributors' brand, one may well doubt that they have the necessary neutrality for a relationship based on confidence. It is basically uncertain whether the distribution sector can play the crucial role of 'infomediary'. Is it in the best position to hold and evaluate information? Furthermore, even if it is represented on the Net, the sector will face a basic conflict of logic. For example, can Fnac simultaneously design a logistical system to fill the shelves of its megastores with books and develop a 'stockless' process to sell books on the Net? The more people actually buy on the Net, the less they will go into traditional retail outlets.

Can the specialist media develop the necessary legitimacy and competence required for the role of 'infomediary'? In view of the success of some car magazines, they would appear to have the capacity to fulfil the role. However, the general public would have to feel that the advice given was not influenced by considerations related to the sale of advertising space. But is the advice of a journalist as valuable as that of a Peugeot engineer? Finally, search engines like Yahoo! have developed a reputation and credibility and should use this to become added-value 'infomediaries'. Others, such as 'kelkoo.com', now No. 1 in Europe, have been created to fulfil this role and become a real shopping guide, rather than simply a price-comparing search engine, a shop-bot.

The 'competence' challenge

Who is better qualified to advise consumers on cosmetics and beauty products: Séphora or Chanel? Usually, and this is said without arrogance or apriorism, competence in the specialist area should be the prerogative of the brand. Only the brand has access to information relating to the 'depth' of the offering, while the distribution sector tends to be more au fait with its 'width' or extent. A Web site offers the opportunity to permanently reinforce this message vis-à-vis consumers (who are themselves increasingly well informed), which is not always possible in a store.

But the consumer is not only looking for information and efficiency in the decision-making process. He or she is also looking for a strong, multisensory experience. Only the brand can add this touch of glamour, indulgence and profusion. Constantly evolving technical skills make it possible to create sites that are not simple information or sales points but points of contact that will reinforce bonds and establish privileged contacts based on the illusion of a one-to-one, personalized relationship between, say, Chanel or Lancôme and the consumer in New York, Stockholm, Paris or London. Each site should offer a truly sensual experience.

At least that is the theory. Sites still need to be designed as a 'live', interactive experience and not just a showcase. Here, 'live' experience means animation, richness of content, colour, ergonomics, ease of access and links, forums for the exchange of ideas, interactivity that makes it possible to personalize communication in the extreme, and the facility to incorporate new information and images on a daily basis.

Few of the sites visited so far meet these criteria. Some take up to a minute to download images which, although beautiful, are mostly fixed and not really interactive. Others present the products but don't differentiate between them for the benefit of individual users.

If users are disappointed by a Web site, they make a note of it and don't return to it. Would anyone think of opening a flagship store on Fifth Avenue without adding the finishing touches? The same applies to a Web site. But since quality is always relative and requirements are shaped by the state of the art on the particular market(s), sites must be constantly improved and updated. It is therefore crucial, when designing the site, that development potential is built in.

The 'living matter' challenge

Before designing a site and being represented on the Internet, it is worth remembering a few basic principles concerning the workings of the network. The Internet is first and foremost an interactive space, a space for development (the possibility for updating sites and information) and creativity (catcher, design, image). Much more so than in online data processing and even more so than in the traditional media, which are naturally fixed in space and time, the 'matter' that forms this network is 'living matter'. This concept of living matter emphasizes the intrinsically developmental and dynamic nature of the content. Becoming part of the Web means adapting to a new form of communication which has nothing to do with the more familiar forms represented by writing, cinema and television. Going online means crossing a technological threshold and sharing a new culture of expression and communication which requires us to free ourselves from the existing frame of reference and learn the language of the Internet. Communication on the Net inverts the traditional process of brand marketing based on advertising. One of the particular features of the Net is that users access it because it is an unrestricted space. They don't log on to receive prefabricated, self-centred messages. This means that servers must be extremely active and interactive. No more fixed presentations: it is vital to have a content that is constantly evolving. The tone can no longer be peremptory, it must be encouraging, with dialogue, suggestions and user participation.

Going online means being judged and compared with other sites in the same sector and all other sectors. The levels of interactivity, development and service offered by the site serve as indicators of the brand's basic client trends.

At a more mundane level, and to finish on the subject of animation, most brands and logos have been created as fixed, two-dimensional images. The Internet adds a third dimension and creates an obligation to provide movement, variety and 'life'. This overturns the hitherto sacrosanct rules governing the intangibility of the brand name. For example, should Renault be written in the same way for all the sites visited: from the most frivolous to the most serious or the corporate? In this respect, brands with a brand icon have an advantage since their 'mouthpiece' can be brought to life in 3D.

Some truths about the new economy

The 'new economy' is here to stay. However big the last fall of the Nasdaq and however buoyant and healthy the 'old' economy, we must recognize that the new economy is not going to go away. But its impact goes beyond the technological sense many gurus talk about. The new economy has radically changed consumer behaviour and expectations. These changes have impacted on all facets of life, even those not related to the Net.

Consumers have acquired new skills and higher expectations through their exposure to the Internet. Services once considered a luxury are now expected as a matter of course, while back in the 'old' economy, these high expectations have created a more demanding consumer, which has affected all sectors of economic life. As a result, old brands will have to change radically if they do not want to irritate or disappoint their regular clients.

In what respects have consumers' expectations changed?

- The Internet has created a culture of participation. Interactivity means participation. Consumers now feel that it is normal to take part in the production or the 'servuction' process. They resent being simply seen as consumers at the end of the value chain.

  The Internet has developed a culture of free expression. The informal style of e-mails, the mix of both distance and proximity encourages individuals to express what they want and this includes brands. Opinion or feedback sites gather the early reactions of innovators or early users of new products. Well-inspired brands encourage the free expression of criticism on their own site.
- The Internet has created a culture of direct access. It flattens organizations, suppresses the intermediates, gives access to once unreachable people. As such, the relationship between organizations and the public has changed. Many brand managers used to see consumers through the tainted glass of focus group rooms or through the survey statistics, as if they feared them. In fact, paradoxically, in the old economy the consumer was much more 'virtual' than he or she is in the new one. Now consumers call direct, they want to get inside the organization. Barriers to entry are useless: it is time to listen to what consumers have to tell us personally and directly.
- The Internet has created a culture of fast response. This began earlier thanks to the competition of direct-mail order catalogues. Some would deliver the goods within two days, then within one day. The e-grocers can now deliver goods soon after the consumer has placed an order. As a consequence, a delivery time of over two days is seen by many consumers as outrageously inefficient, even in the bricks-and-mortar world.
- The Internet has led to what someone nicely termed the 'truth economy'. It is impossible to see cracks on a Web site: such behaviour would encourage viral countermarketing, and other angry collective and 'contagious' reactions. The Internet is the medium of the consumer by which they interact and also unite. This runs counter to the present domination of the mass media and advertising.

- The Internet has developed a 'me' culture. Consumers are treated as individuals – respect and individuality are now taken for granted on the Internet. Well-designed sites recognize us and greet us at each new click. Such expectations do not disappear in the old economy. Failing to meet these new expectations creates frustration and discontent among consumers. To summarize, the Internet has fostered a culture of personalized service and proactive care. Certainly, it is a big challenge for any brand in the old economy. Consumers will not lower their expectations when they are not on the Internet. Hence, the old economy will have to upgrade its service accordingly.

Is your brand 'mediactive'?

What is the impact of the Internet on the skills that brands will have to develop? One of the most significant is that it is the end of 'canned' information. Companies used to deliver canned information (catalogues, leaflets, brochures, annual reports, even CD ROMS, etc...) to the market. Web sites accentuate the convergence between brands and media. A Web site will foster repeat usage only if it is newsworthy. This means that managing a brand on the Internet is akin to managing any media: change is the rule, news is the key. To paraphrase the words of the Internet guru J F Variot: 'mediactivity' will become a necessity for tomorrow's brands. This means a constant flow of new information and services streamed through a Web magazine, an online catalogue, an interactive demo, an FAQ corner, pedagogy, tele-maintenance. Even humour or games will have to have a place in this 'mediactive' space.

Is your brand hyper-relational?

Relationship marketing was a buzzword of the 1990s. The Internet brings the concept many steps further. It will not suffice to wish to establish long-term relationships, the brand will have to be hyper-relational. It will have to use the latest technologies to propose the best after-sales service, the best CRM (Customer relationship marketing). The brand will have to demonstrate it is permanently hearing the consumer and that it is quick to react. Proactivity will be the ideal. Hyper-personalization also has implications for tailoring consumer e-magazines, or e-mails, or offers. The hyper-relational brand must demonstrate that it is open to true dialogue. Finally the brand must be a permanent learner: surveying, auditing, profiling its customer base and updating its knowledge for an adaptive and updated response to consumers' expectations.

Is your brand connective?

The essence of the Internet, as its name indicates, is that it allows people to gather according to their interests. To succeed on the Internet, brands will have to espouse this very basic function. This is a difficult task because it necessitates a radical shift in orientation. Instead of speaking of itself, the brand should first speak of the other (the internaut), and his or her own lifestyle, values and interests. The brand should also foster virtual communities, tied by some common interest, which is rarely the brand itself. For example, babies and childcare may be a common interest but not the Huggies brand. The role of the connective brand is to provide virtual spaces for these communities of interest, bringing relevant information when needed, but not commercial information about the brand itself.

Finally, the connective brand will exploit one of the basic principles of the Internet: partnerships. It is amazing to see how, unlike in the old economy, e-brands do develop partnerships with other brands, even with competitors (through the creation of a marketplace for example).

part two

Brand practices in question

ten

The tendency towards decapitalization

If a brand is the capital of a company, then it is logical to suppose that every marketing campaign should capitalize on the name of this brand. Well known though this may be, it is worth restating once again.

An observation of brand policy implementation reveals a paradox. The 'brands are the company's capital' mantra is an oft-repeated one, yet in reality decapitalization is everywhere. Office whiteboards and flip charts are covered with brand architecture diagrams showing the mother brand reigning supreme at the top, and the daughter brands appearing below in what is therefore a subsidiary position. However, even the briefest examination of product packaging or advertising reveals the actual truth. Generally speaking, the emphasis is on the daughter brand, and the so-called 'mother' brand can be allocated even less space than the basic minimum taken up by merely endorsing brands.

In the long term, though, the mother brand is the name that matters, for it carries the value or 'brand equity'. The purpose of products and daughter brands is to make the mother brand increasingly attractive by linking it with current trends, modern needs and emerging markets. However, their lifespan is not infinite. Yoplait products, for example, have an ultra-short lifecycle of two to three years at the most.

The decapitalization instinct

First of all, it has to be admitted that there is a strong instinctive tendency towards decapitalization which is deplored in theory but practised unconsciously.

In the mobile telecommunications sector, new entrants – such as Orange and One 2 One – aggressively organize their communications strategy entirely around their respective names. In their attempts to build a reputation as quickly as possible, they have avoided creating daughter brands, instead using clear, friendly descriptors such as 'Just Talk', 'Orange Net', Orange Wap', 'boxed and ready' as names for their innovative services. At the same time, there is a rampant decapitalization at incumbent operators. A case in point is France Télécom which invested millions of euros in advertising in favour of increasingly independent daughter brands such as Ola, Loft and Mobicarte, each addressing a specific target. Itineris, the former mobile telephone flagship brand, was relegated to the status of 'label brand' – a euphemism for lowering its profile, which had the immediate effect of reducing the level of brand awareness. The France Télécom name itself became more and more discreet on the Ola, Loft and Mobicarte packaging, despite the fact that France Télécom is one of the best-known and most popular brands in France. In failing to capitalize on this fact, the company was effectively forfeiting an extremely useful competitive advantage in a climate of rapid deregulation.

When Dim came under the ownership of the American Sara Lee group, its new parent company implemented segmentation – which was a good thing – and created daughter brands to identify the different products for the various segments; these included brands such as Macadam, Sublim and Diam's. Inspection of the advertising revealed that these daughter brands enjoyed pride of place, while the Dim logo was relegated to the bottom right-hand corner of advertising posters or magazine pages. Decapitalization was at work once again.

Miscalculations

One of the immediate consequences of decapitalization is a reduction in the share of voice, a fact concealed by the usual calculations. The traditional method of calculating the advertising share of voice of a brand is to add together total expenditure on its daughter brands: Sublim, Macadam and Diam's for Dim, or Ola, Loft and Mobicarte for France Télécom. This is a miscalculation. It is true that, from an accounting point of view, the company does indeed generate these sums. However, seen from the point of view of the consumer, who perceives less and less of a connection between these daughter brands and the mother brand as the latter's advertising saliency decreases, these campaigns are disjointed and do not serve to build a strong, united brand with modern, up-to-date resonances. They cannot, therefore, simply be added together. Inevitably, this creates a share of voice imbalance between the budgets of the new operators on the one hand and the much smaller and individually calculated budgets of Ola, Loft and Mobicarte.

Why this systematic shift?

How is this systematic decapitalization to be explained? A psychoanalyst may contend that there is an unfortunate subtext to the term 'mother brand': freedom is achieved only by breaking the umbilical connection to the mother brand, and thus a gap is created. Another explanation is perhaps the failure to appreciate the need to continue supporting the mother brand. Within the company itself, the brand is so familiar that it becomes practically indistinguishable from the walls and furniture. Energy is – laudably – poured into innovation, but there is no sense of the constant importance of nurturing the mother brand on which the entire edifice is built. Innovation is a vital 'resource' for the mother brand, and so ways to fuel it into the mother brand image must be developed.

A further explanation is the underestimation of the power of the mother brand and the respect it commands outside the company. When a brand and a company share a single name, discontentment with obstacles, slowness and inertia within the company reflect themselves in the attitudes of individual employees and teams towards the company's name. In this way, 'back office' grievances are wrongly projected on to the brand itself, which clients perceive as the company's 'front office'. This malady afflicts many large companies undergoing internal change.

Accidents sometimes provide an insight into the power of the brand, which may have been forgotten. In 1997 Fleury-Michon, a leader in the quality ready-to-eat food sector, attempted to segment its product range, increasing the emphasis on its line of top-quality ham by using the Les Fleurons name. One change was a small reduction in the size of the box containing the words 'Fleury-Michon' on the product packaging, making the Les Fleurons name stand out more. The result was immediate: sales fell. Clients and sales were lost through even the smallest decrease in the mother brand's visual impact.

There are also cultural factors at work behind the decapitalization instinct. In many organizations, individuals identify more with their division, branch or department than with the institution itself. Researchers at France Télécom describe themselves as working for CNET. The young sales team headhunted from the big marketing companies by France Télécom identified to such an extent with their fight to penetrate the fast-moving consumer goods (FMCG) sector that they saw themselves more as FTM (M stands for 'Mobile') than France Télécom – a company that seemed very distant to them, immersed as they were in the competitive world of hypermarkets and large specialist outlets.

Competition: a rude awakening

In general, competitors often prompt the realization that rampant decapitalization is at work. In this way L'Oréal, competing against Nivea, which had just begun to implement a systematic, worldwide brand extension policy centred entirely on its own name, in which the only daughter brands permitted were more or less self-descriptive (Nivea Visage, Nivea Beauty, etc), received a lesson in the limitations of its so far discreet approach. L'Oréal had, after all, concentrated its advertising focus on brands such as Plénitude, Elnett, Progress and Studio Line, each operating as a fully autonomous entity. Where was the L'Oréal brand amid this proliferation? Nowhere. It had been left on the corporate shelf.

So how did L'Oréal respond to Nivea's innovation? Plénitude was certainly innovative, as were Progress and Elnett; but where innovation is divided, its impact is reduced. It was time to rediscover the added value by returning to its source: L'Oréal Paris. Company advertising now proclaims, 'L'Oréal innove' ('A L'Oréal Innovation') whenever the Plénitude range – or any other daughter brand – is extended. The hierarchy has at last been restored in company advertising, packaging and – in all likelihood – at an internal level.

L'Oréal Paris has adopted an interesting approach to recapitalizing in advertising, in which statements and announcements concerning new products from Plénitude, Progress or any other daughter brand are made by L'Oréal itself. Visually, each campaign is similar: in fact, there is just one campaign in which each product is distinguishable by the respective top model hired. The L'Oréal Paris name, with its one distinctive signature – 'Because I'm worth it' – now frames the products from above and below. We sense that value creation is intentionally being attached to the suprabrand itself. An examination of 25 years of advertising for Dior's Eau Sauvage also reveals a sudden change of direction in 1989. After 22 years of advertising the Eau Sauvage name in large letters (compared to the discreet Christian Dior) on the product advertising, the order was brusquely changed: nowadays Christian Dior takes precedence over a discreet Eau Sauvage. A recapitalization had indeed been long overdue. Which name has the long-term value? Dior. The lower Dior's profile in the advertising, the lower the company's profile in terms of general relevance and modernity at a time when new brands seemed to monopolize and symbolize the concept of modernity in the eyes of new generations. In the world youth market, Dior is competing not against Chanel or Guerlain, but Calvin Klein... It is time to make 'Dior' more meaningful to teenagers.

Horizontal communication

The previous case reminds us that a mother-brand is not constructed solely through daughter brands, a fact observed by the management of Renault: the brand's image suffered in a number of areas when compared to its European competitors, such as Volkswagen. Image is a major factor in determining buyer discounts; a potential Volkswagen client negotiates less over discount. Image also influences a car's price positioning.

Paradoxically, the image of Renault's cars, which have scored spectacular sales successes, is better than that of the brand itself. Consequently, the daughter brands have done less than expected to promote the mother brand, with the communication emphasis placed solely (with the exception of Formula One) on advertising individual models. In reality, this prevents rapid capitalization and puts the brand at a disadvantage compared to its competitors. The logic of capitalization demands large-scale budgets and horizontal campaigns on the brand itself, which will have repercussions on the way in which communication and operations are organized within the company. The brand should drive product communications.

Capitalizing on products, too

The automobile industry provides other examples of 'rampant decapitalization', but these are linked to the brands of the individual models themselves. Take, for example, Peugeot's well-known model numbering system.

The first digit indicates the position within the range; the third digit identifies the generation... while the 0 symbolizes the space originally left for the starting handle hole! The impeccable logic of this system dictates that the 206 must replace the legendary 205, with each new version being assigned a number one increment up from its predecessor. This numeric system gives each new model a youthful feel and emphasises the innovative aspect of the Peugeot brand – an area in which, like any other major brand, it must be strong. However, this logic also has a hidden cost, thus far unidentified but none the less real for that: it annuls all previous investment in creating an image around the previous model's name. Having built a reputation for its 205, a brand new one had to be created for the 206, which meant fresh advertising investment; although, fortunately, not entirely from scratch. Also, when the last digit of one model in the range is higher than that of the other models, it appears to age all the other models; and yet there is no reason why '205' could not have been used in the same way as

Chanel's No. 5, Kronenbourg's 1664 or Volkswagen's Golf. The Golf is now 25 years old and in its fifth incarnation. The Japanese have long been masters of this concept, capitalizing on brands that have defied time: the Honda Civic and the Toyota Corolla have plenty of life left in them yet. In any case – to return to Peugeot – this Sisyphean system will have to end one day: what will happen when the tenth generation is launched? What number will follow 209?

eleven

So where is your brand strong?

A brand may be an intangible asset but – as we have seen in Chapter 4 – we should never forget its tangible origins. Indeed, we should go yet further and reflect that, for customers who enjoy the luxury of choice, the question today is no longer one of quality: in too many mature markets, all remaining competitors offer very good quality. Is Michelin really better than Goodyear? Is it true that Firestone produces inferior tyres? And if there genuinely is a quality differential between Continental and Uniroyal, does it really reflect the price differential?

Today, a brand has to be perceived as an authority on some strong point. In other words, it must have a tangible feature that sets the standard in its market and generates fascinated and enthusiastic word of mouth among its target group.

Authority cannot, therefore, be something vague or intangible: it has to be concrete. It can be based on an aspect of the product, a consumer benefit or – as is increasingly the case in mature markets – service levels, consumer experience or a vision. How many brands can define their strong point in a few succinct words? Hardly any.

From the concrete to the abstract

We should bear in mind that research on the image of mega-brands reveals a crucial fact which is somehow overlooked. Not all products associated with a particular brand by consumers play an equal part in forming the image of that mega-brand. Some products carry the exact characteristics of the brand that they portray – the word 'portrait' is in fact derived from the French words *'porter'* (to carry) and *'trait'* (characteristic). These particularly representative products are known as 'prototypes' – not in the sense of test versions, but rather the best examples of the brand. These are products which are central to the perception of the brand.

Table 11.1 below illustrates the key role played by prototype products in the image of the Danone brand, a typical mega-brand by the width of its product range.

As the table shows, the image gap between product and brand grows as the product becomes increasingly atypical of the brand. Prototypes are in fact products whose image gap with their founding brand (measured over 10 or so items) is effectively close to zero. Since the brand itself does not precede these products, it may logically be deduced that these products have in fact been responsible for shaping the collective representation of the brand they carry.

The prototype concept does not always refer to a product in the range: it may be a particular skill, an overall characteristic (for example, the profusion of colours used in a cosmetics brand such as Bourjois) or an individual, as in the case of Virgin. What is therefore important is not to lose sight of the fact that from a consumer point of view, there is something tangible at the heart of the brand. When questioned about a brand, consumers usually begin by describing it in terms of the typical product or service it offers, and then go on to mention the strong point of this product or service. Intangible associations follow after this.

Curiously, we pay too little attention to the consumer, whose first statement is apparently disregarded: the majority of qualitative

Table 11.1 How a mega-brand's image is built: Danone
Source: Kapferer and Laurent, 1998

	Gap between product image and Danone's image	
Which products most typify Danone? (scale of 1–10)	Danette (9.33)	1.72
	Plain yoghurt (9.16)	1.97
Which products typify Danone a little less? (scale of 1–10)	Fromage Blanc (8.01)	7.25
	Liégeois (8.07)	8.50

Table 11.2 Image gap between two mega-brands: the case of Philips and Brandt. *Source:* Kapferer and Laurent, 1998
(1 = strong association to the item; 3 = weak association)

	Brandt	Philips	Image gap [Brandt–Philips]
Modern	1.34	1.33	[0.01]
Good quality	1.47	1.51	[0.04]
A brand which understands women	1.69	1.65	[0.04]
Easy to use	1.28	1.34	[0.06]
Technology	1.63	1.53	[0.10]
Reassuring	1.60	1.47	[0.22]
Low price	2.04	2.16	[0.12]
Liked by family	1.20	1.36	[0.16]
Gadget	2.51	2.32	[0.19]
Durable	1.36	1.55	[0.19]
On consumer's wavelength	2.02	1.82	[0.20]
ELECTRICAL APPLIANCE SPECIALIST	1.24	1.50	[0.26]
Advertising	1.72	1.43	[0.20]
Proud to own one	2.14	1.81	[0.33]
Progressive	1.76	1.39	[0.37]
REFRIGERATION SPECIALIST	1.42	1.82	[0.40]
Desirable	2.45	2.03	[0.42]
Innovation	1.97	1.53	[0.44]
COOKING APPLIANCE SPECIALIST	1.43	1.93	[0.50]
LIGHT ELECTRICAL GOODS SPECIALIST	2.08	1.51	[0.57]
WASHING EQUIPMENT SPECIALIST	1.20	1.86	[0.66]
TV/HI-FI SPECIALIST	2.01	1.14	[0.87]

studies concentrate on analysing his or her second statement. However, the bedrock of the brand remains the product or service and its strong point. A brand whose concrete strong point cannot be identified by consumers is in fact a fragile brand. After all, even though they may be persuaded to buy a brand for its image or status or badge value, consumers seek to rationalize their choice: they want to be able to explain their choice in terms of superiority.

They may refer to the comfort of the latest Nike or Salomon products or describe Virgin Atlantic in terms of its service, like Saturn or Dell. It's time we started listening to the consumer.

Table 11.2 demonstrates the image gap between two mega-brands – Philips and Brandt. What does it tell us? Contrary to received wisdom, there is in fact very little differentiation between these two mega-brands in terms of their intangible image, that fundamental component of communication which is the subject of endless days of deliberation by advertising agencies. Brandt, a regional leader, says in its advertising 'Watching your children grow'. Philips' slogan is now 'Let's make things better'. However, a differentiation really appears in the skill-related section at the bottom of the table: customers perceive very precise areas of authority, expertise, for each of the brands. They are able to identify the strong point of each brand.

So where is your brand strong? Where is it an acknowledged authority?

twelve

Unveil all your values!

When the Peugeot 406 was launched, it was observed during a discussion with Peugeot management that the car had a special feature: it was one of the most recyclable cars – if not the most recyclable – on the market. This information was simply omitted from the publicity material, mailshots and exhibition stands. It was, however, buried deep inside the product brochure.

Such modesty, given modern insistence that brands must defend their added value, is astonishing. Naturally, we are by no means suggesting that recyclability is the overriding concern of most European consumers and should therefore constitute the main thrust of the 406's advertising positioning: in Southern Europe (unlike Germany or Sweden), the environment has not yet become a key factor on which to base purchasing decisions.

Yet French manufacturers have too long been accused of lagging behind their German counterparts (who are always cited as leaders in this field) on this issue. Such modesty is therefore inexplicable.

Our position in such cases is clear: wherever a brand advantage is a source of value, it should be promoted. Sadly, this advice runs contrary to the practices and methods currently monopolizing brand and product communication.

The limits of the USP

Advertisers have learnt to focus on one unique and repetitive promise: the unique selling proposition, a doctrine driven by the stealthy nature of advertising exposure. The slogan for the 406 is 'You'll never have to choose between pleasure and safety again'. This positioning angle is satisfactory enough per se. However, it leaves little room for advertising the new model's advanced ecological benefits, which contradict the perception that the Peugeot brand is a little behind its German competitors in this respect. Knowing that, so far, the strategic emphasis Peugeot placed on its diesel engine (which was the subject of considerable scorn at the time, but has now become much more widely accepted) served to erode the company's 'green' reputation, such an omission was really counterproductive. There was an urgent need to provide an extra factual proof to the perception of the 'green' 406, if not the Peugeot brand as a whole.

Communication is not just about advertising. Nowadays, value is created by utilizing and promoting every source of value. The USP logic reveals the domination of advertising thinking on all the communications. It's time we turned this proposition on its head. If a piece of information is worth mentioning, it must be mentioned: the only negotiables are its target, its medium and the timescale.

Each value identifies its own target

Traditional demand-driven marketing teaches us that we should first identify the target and then devise a suitable message to reach it. The value approach dictates a supply-based marketing strategy. If your car happens to be environmentally friendly, you should devise a micro-marketing programme to inform everyone who values this feature: local authorities, consumer associations, young people, ecology groups, etc. Perhaps your TV commercials need to be adapted appropriately for transmission during programmes that attract an ecologically conscious audience. In any event, the environmental features should be clearly identified in the product brochure which you supply on request to all prospective customers and also, of course, on the product's Web site. The Internet's great strength is its ability to create instant connections between the consumer's own area of interest and the attributes of the desired model.

Identifying a range of micro-targets in this way is undeniably a complicated process. But these targets are generally better-informed and more influential, and therefore generate word of mouth and positive rumours (Kapferer, 1991). This plays such a major role in a car purchasing decision that all word-of-mouth networks must be saturated with involving credible information. Involved consumers are proselytes, if not opinion formers.

Rediscovering opinion formers

L'Oréal organizes its brands according to distribution channel and sales type. For example, the skincare brand to be found in chemists' stores is La Roche Posay, which is sold virtually on prescription. Vichy used to be the big general-purpose name in skin cosmetics, and was sold freely over the counter. But is it possible to be a major brand in the health sector without ever involving the skincare specialist, that oracle of the world of healthcare? Until recently, only the La Roche Posay 'medical' brand utilized such an approach. Breaking with decades of received wisdom that 'over-the-counter' sales meant no visits to health professionals, Vichy decided to create a specific 'information force' who would visit skincare specialists. Its aim was not to achieve prescription status, but rather to promote the benefits of its products in order to obtain favourable attitudes or even passive goodwill. After all, Vichy's products are backed by L'Oréal's finest research work, and the benefits of this should be promoted to everyone who appreciates such facts. This means that all brands have a duty to consider the opinion leaders who shape consumer opinion: Danone, for example, uses its Foundation to nurture nutritionists and dieticians. However, the 'opinion former' concept must not be restricted to parties with a purely professional interest in the product or service. In practice, we turn to friends and relatives on a whole range of matters because they seem more knowledgeable than we are, which makes us value their opinion. Sociologically, they are virtually identical to us (and this is precisely what makes them so easily accessible): they seem to have a closer involvement in a particular area than we do, and thus they become micro-experts. What distinguishes them from 'the man in the street' is their knowledge and access to information. They are often also major consumers of that product category. The philosophy of value creation holds that the brand must operate an information strategy to involve and inform this group, recognizing their special status and influence. The Internet is the perfect medium for feeding their insatiable appetite for news on the brand, its products, its origins and its philosophy. They should also be involved and recognized as opinion formers by the brand (Rosen, 2001).

Public image, private image

As we have seen, modern technology provides new solutions to the problem of communicating with opinion formers. Until recently, this 'private image' (in the sense of 'private club') could be created only via consumer magazines, and did not correspond to the public image perceived by the rest of the market. Opinion formers should be recognized as such, and supplied positive promotional information in advance.

The advent of the super-database now makes it possible to communicate with this target group. Leaders tend to inform themselves better: they know where to find information and have the motivation to do so. Consumer magazines such as *Danoé*, which are distributed to micro-target group leaders using huge customer databases, play a direct role in this selective information distribution strategy. The ultimate goal of these informational databases and relationship marketing programmes – to increase per household sales volumes – may be the same, but their importance in unveiling value is paramount.

thirteen

Aim for the critical size

It has been almost impossible over the last few years to ignore the far-reaching consequences of the concept of critical size. Many intellectually appealing marketing proposals founder when faced with a simple consideration: has the brand reached the critical size necessary to compete, communicate and survive amid wider competition? Yesterday's strategies, with their clear demarcations of brand territory and subtle organization of brand/market pairs, carefully positioning each brand in its own slot in the portfolio, have been swept aside by pragmatism, realism and the demands of modern competition, which in the first instance require critical size.

Such questions of scale are not only references to mega-mergers of distributors which command that manufacturers be still more capable of flexing their considerable muscles in their dealings with such distributive giants. Size, which had previously been an indicator of success – after all, how many companies remain small by choice? – now becomes an essential prerequisite for success. This is not, however, because expansion flatters managers' egos: an examination of the facts shows that size produces a series of quantitative rachet effects which gives the leading brands an additional competitive advantage and explains their improved profitability.

The link between threshold effects and size

Consumer research reveals a few interesting size-related benefits which are still relatively unrecognized and enjoyed mainly by the leaders.

The first of these concerns the 'threshold effect' with regard to spontaneous brand awareness, which is considered by most marketing managers as one of the key requirements for a strong brand. Spontaneous awareness is proof of an almost instantaneous association to the product category. Our analysis of more than 50 of the most diverse product categories reveals that on average, consumers spontaneously name three brands (Laurent, Kapferer and Roussel, 1990). If we eliminate the No. 1 and No. 2 brands, this leaves only one slot for all other brands. This is why challenger brands are faced with stagnating spontaneous awareness, despite continued growth in their aided awareness. This translates into a prominently kinked curve representing the relationship between spontaneous recall and aided awareness, as shown in the following illustration (Figure. 13.1).

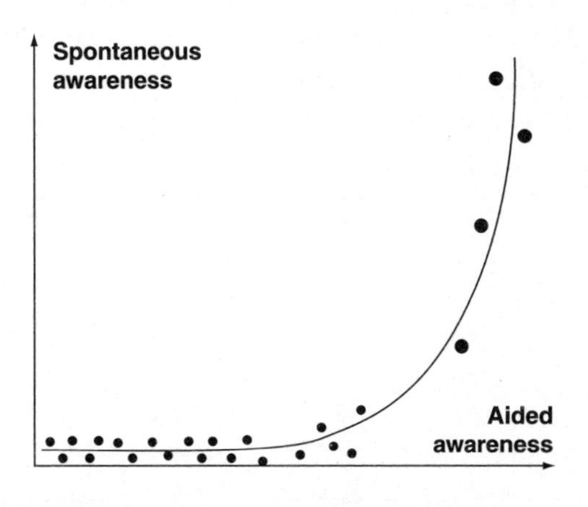

Figure 13.1 Threshold effect in brand awareness
(*Source:* Laurent, Kapferer and Roussel, 1990)

The practical outcome is that, in all markets where there are strong leaders, the brand has to reach a very high threshold of aided awareness before it can have any hope of eventually seeing growth in its spontaneous awareness – which gives the market leaders a considerable advantage.

The second effect favouring the larger brands, and the market leader in particular, is the 'memory bias' enjoyed by the best-known names. When consumers are asked which brands they have purchased recently, they tend to name well-known brands. A trivial point? Tellingly, the conversion rate (declared purchasing divided by awareness) increases constantly with brand awareness, as shown in Table 13.1.

In short, the figures suggest that the consumer's recall of recent purchasing increases with the brand's awareness. Consumers were more likely to name better-known brands as their most recent purchases, which increases the likelihood of repeat purchases in a low- involvement purchase situation. However, this is not to suggest that there is no market share without brand awareness: the leading Scotch whisky in French hypermarkets is not Ballantines, Johnny Walker or J&B, but William Peel, with an advertising spend of zero.

The third effect favouring strong brands was suggested by A Ehrenberg. This British researcher, analysing only panel data (and thus behaviour), found that as a brand's market penetration increased, so did customer loyalty and per consumer volumes (see also page 173). He coined the term 'double jeopardy' to describe this empirical and reliable finding.

It is no surprise that firms try to take advantage of this by striving for returns of scale.

Table 13.1 Declared purchases and brand awareness

Brand (Product category – ham)	Brand Awareness	Purchase Declared	Conversion rate P/A
Herta	90%	45%	50%
Fleury-Michon	86%	32%	37%
Madrange	80%	28%	35%
Olida	77%	19%	24%
Paul Prédault	76%	20%	26%
Aoste	63%	18%	28%
Géo	50%	11%	22%
Jean Caby	28%	5%	18%

A revolution in brand portfolios

These figures have a practical effect on how multi-brand portfolios are managed, with efficiency being rated above structural sophistication. This revolution is typified by the example of the Domaxel group.

Domaxel is France's leading group of independent DIY retailers and France's No. 3 distributor of DIY and household equipment. It operated a five-brand portfolio:

- Bricosphère, with an average floorspace of 1,200 square metres per store, and conceptually similar to most other large home improvement and DIY superstores;
- Maison Conseil, combining the male world of DIY and the female world of decoration. Average floorspace is 850 square metres;
- Bricorelais, a local store franchise for town centres (550 square metres);
- the Dompro network, targeting professionals;
- the Manufrance chain of stores.

Today, a group's strength is not in the sum of its various market shares or the volumes commanded by each line or brand: it is in the intrinsic strength of its brands. This makes it misleading to describe Domaxel as the No. 3 distributor after Castorama and Leroy-Merlin: none of its individual 'brands' or lines is strong. Would it be then possible to group 600 retailers together under a common banner? No, according to all the distribution textbooks: it is a basic rule of good management that you cannot give one umbrella name to a collection of disparate retail outlets, far less to a range of store identities each representing specific concepts.

Management is the art of the possible. When fighting two giants such as Castorama and Leroy-Merlin, can you afford to take a purist approach? Surely the point is to flex your muscles – not, as before, via the straightforward mechanism of the single purchasing agency, but this time as a decisive, customer-driven market force? This is precisely what happened in 1999, when it was decided to bring all of the group's retail outlets together under the unifying name of Weldom. This simple name-change alone increased sales turnover by nearly 10 per cent.

The hotel business is another example of a case in which competitive considerations should now come first. The Hôtel et Compagnie group controlled three hotel chains, each with its own market sector positioning:

- Nuit d'Hôtel, with 45 hotels, competes with Formule 1 in the so-called 'no-star' budget hotel sector. It differentiates itself through the fact that each of its rooms has its own toilets and washbasins, although its shower facilities are shared;
- Balladins (77 hotels), at the top end of the one-star sector, offers comparable hotel and restaurant facilities to those provided by Etap Hôtel (105 hotels);
- Climat de France (158 hotels) is positioned in the two-star hotel sector alongside competitors such as Ibis and Campanile (285 and 310 hotels respectively).

What use is distinctiveness if, though a lack of promotion, it goes unrecognized? Why bother to make a good impression without a dense national network to create loyalty? In 1999, Hôtel et Compagnie were quickly forced to concede that the rules of the game had changed.

Formule 1 knew this. The inventor of the new zero-star segment had set out to achieve critical mass (300 hotels) very rapidly to recoup a sizeable advertising budget and establish itself as the dominant leader and point of reference in its market. Assuming an advertising spend of 10 euros per room per month, Ibis – with its 20,000 rooms – could also have raised over 2 million euros. However, with a mere 9,000 rooms, Climat de France could only have invested 1 million euros. One chain was in a position to consider television advertising; the other was not. What chance was there for Balladins – to say nothing of Nuit d'Hôtel? There was no doubt as to the quality of the product, but they were weak brands: a unifying strategy was needed. Surely it would be a better idea to capitalize around a single brand by grouping the Nuit d'Hôtel hotels under the Balladins Express banner as a Balladins sub-brand? After all, the world leader Holiday Inn capitalizes around its single brand, but differentiates its products using names such as Holiday Inn Express, Holiday Inn Garden Court, etc.

The trend towards capitalizing to achieve threshold effects is not a new one, but has been growing in speed and prominence. The Labeyrie brand realized it stood no chance of promoting its individual identity as long as it restricted its market to *foie gras*, a product which was affected by seasonality. Extending the brand to include salmon and duck breast fillets allowed it to reach the size necessary to justify recognition-building budgets and television advertising.

Claude Bébéar was an early master of the critical size concept. Since creating the AXA insurance group, he has worked tirelessly to phase out the names of the insurance companies he has bought. Who in each country now remembers the names of these companies, despite the fact that they were market leader for many years? AXA systematically implements the same policy at international level when it buys out well-known local insurance companies. After a very short transition period, their name is replaced by AXA's. This is how the Equitable name disappeared in the United States, Prudential in Germany, etc.

AXA has good reasons for pursuing such a policy, one of which is the desire to establish its new corporate culture within these companies immediately. The other reason is globalization.

The demands of 'market space'

Insurance companies trade on reassuring factors such as their reputation and long-term credibility. The power of their name is intended as a guarantee that they will still be in existence a century from now. Today, however, power is measured in terms of worldwide profile. Big is beautiful. Insurance brands no longer compete on a local level, but in what is known as 'market space' – that immediate and boundless domain of international communication – via such media as fax, Reuter's, CNN, Bloomberg and the Internet. The price of admission to this select group is steep: only 'world-class' brands are welcome. At the same time, what AXA is selling is a relationship, a listening ear and an advisory service for customers. This is why a direct, face-to-face relationship with the insurer remains necessary. It scarcely matters that Equitable in the United States or Prudential in Germany should disappear as brands if the scale and scope which this confers on AXA gradually draws the group into the exclusive circle of world brands, all the while preserving the sense of continuity and intimacy of the 'local' service – either face to face or through interactive communication, and the Internet. Think global, act local!

The distinction between 'market space' and 'market place' is a fundamental one (Raypont and Sviokla, 1994). 'Market space' refers to the concept of a competitive domain which is now totally open and indivisible, and operates through the circulation of images, information and communication. Brands must appreciate that they are now competing on the open field of world signs and symbols. 'Market place' stems from the fact that tangible, material services remain subject to national regulations, local cultures and distribution issues. These two areas call for specific managerial approaches. AXA's strength is that it gives its local subsidiaries a great degree of freedom to optimize their services and relationships in the 'market place' and to maintain an entrepreneurial culture. The symbolic issues, however, can never be localized or divided: there is only one AXA brand image worldwide. It is managed at the corporate level.

Redefining brand leadership

Creating a mega-brand requires an understanding of consumers' points of view. How do they themselves define a mega-brand? Is it a segment-leading brand, like Ariel in the European detergent market? The brand manager may be satisfied with Ariel's performance and market share, but do consumers perceive Ariel as a major brand which commands respect? Do they admire the brand's 30 years of commitment to them? As long as Ariel suggests nothing more than a detergent, the chances are that they do not. To build a mega-brand, you have to broaden your horizons and move beyond the scope of the initial product category. One immediate advantage to this approach is that it promotes humility: a 15 per cent share in the detergent market translates into a more modest figure once the category or reference market is broadened to include, say, clothing care or household care. By redefining success, we give the brand new ambitions and a new development framework – especially when it comes to services, which are now a necessary lever in brand value. In so doing, we also redefine company organization.

fourteen

Brand image does not equal brand usage

Does the name Sergio Zyman mean anything to you? This Mexican national, nicknamed 'Aya Cola', was the brilliant senior vice-president of the Coca-Cola Beverage Company until May 1998. In his recent book about Coca-Cola's extraordinary growth (he increased sales of Coke from 10 billion to 15 billion cases per year over a five-year period), one phrase recurs constantly: 'We owe our success to the fact that we've never forgotten the aim of Coca-Cola: to get the largest possible number of people to drink the largest possible quantity of Coke at the highest possible price, so that the company will make even more money' (Zyman, 1999).

This exceptionally forthright statement has the advantage of drawing attention to Coca-Cola's key growth strategy: to get people who already drink Coke to consume yet more. The directness of his approach will no doubt disquiet advocates of relationship marketing, who are more at home with the carefully nuanced language of building long-term relationships and establishing a rapport with the consumer. This is not an attempt to contrast these two points of view, but rather a reminder that per capita volume must be a major preoccupation when building brand value. Naturally, we must increase the image and profile of the brand: these are goals of undeniable importance. However, it is easy to name well-known and well-loved brands whose creative advertising enjoys critical acclaim but still fails to lift sales beyond a certain ceiling. We must therefore use appropriate tools to tackle the problem of per capita volume growth. Image may influence behaviour, but there are other specific leverages too. Additionally, unlike the luxury products sector (in which consumption creates disillusion and erodes dreams), consumption in the consumer goods market breeds proximity, familiarity and habit – in other words, loyalty. Increasing brand usage is thus another way of boosting brand equity, the financial value of the brand.

Sadly, per capita volume is far from being a key consideration in the marketing plans of many brands. Why not?

Barriers to the volume mentality

Today, having learnt the lessons of all the studies conducted into the link between profitability and loyalty, companies have adjusted their marketing objectives: less conquest, more loyalty. The modern strategy is now to increase brand share in each consumer's purchasing decision and to raise the brand's selection score (how many times out of a hundred purchases will a single consumer choose to purchase our brand?). Loyalty programmes and promotions based on repeat purchases are useful, as is direct promotion of the brand values, which can be individually targeted using databases or a genuinely interactive Web site (Pointillart, 1996).

All the same, marketing plans that focus primarily on a systematic increase in volume per capita are something of a rarity.

There are cultural reasons for this. The more one follows the current fashion of describing the consumer as a 'friend' who should be addressed not as a consumer but as an individual, the more outdated the notion of persuading him to buy even more seems.

However, in mature markets such as ours, growth depends on intensive rather than extensive strategies. Brand value (and thus company value) can only be accumulated by creating a more intense link between the brand and each of its consumers. It is all well and good for the brand to be loved and understood and for its benefits and deep values to be expounded in the process, but if the relationship remains a platonic one, it will create no value for the shareholder. It will not generate added consumption. We are all familiar with brands which generate sky-high levels of empathy, or are backed by advertising which is adored by consumers, yet continue to languish amid desperately flat per capita sales.

The problem is that per capita volume does not increase automatically along with greater brand esteem or an improved image. It is often quite the opposite: in this case, behaviour comes before attitude. Despite this, marketing teams consider it more profitable to work on the relationship between the brand and the customer than to increase volume.

The second problem with the per capita volume approach is that it is not mentioned in most basic marketing information sources. How many companies or brands are in the habit of segmenting the market along two dimensions: the brand's rate of consumption, (low, medium, high) and the brand's rate of selection? Brand studies to date have generally been based on a different type of segmentation: psychographic, socio-demographic or a simple distinction between buyers and non-buyers. The volume approach is hampered in the short term by an information barrier. Qualitative market research agencies do not, by definition, adopt a behavioural approach. They prefer to stick to their strengths – the quest for the essential character and inherent essence of the brand.

The volume approach – which entails a re-examination of the data from a volume per capita standpoint – is thus bound to signal a cultural revolution in the qualitative and quantitative research conducted by the company and its partners.

The same is true of the advertising agencies. Although advertising investment has a positive effect on volumes overall, this objective should be included among the criteria for evaluating the quality of copy or of a campaign. It is, for example, significant that all Coca-Cola's TV and cinema advertising features someone actually drinking the product and appearing refreshed and satisfied. These adverts all portray consumption of the brand in one way or another. Current posters for 7-Up feature the word 'Thirsty' in large letters. The Coca-Cola and Pepsi companies are both focused on consumption.

Building the strategic volume matrix

All brands need a precise understanding of how their consumers fit into the strategic volume matrix. This has two axes: the rate of consumption and the rate of selection.

Rate of brand selection per household

Volume per capita:	LOW	MEDIUM	HIGH
LOW			
MEDIUM			
HIGH			

Figure 14.1 Strategic matrix for implementation of the volume approach

By combining these two dimensions (each of which is subdivided into low, medium and high levels), we define eight behavioural segments which are useful in studying how to make the volume grow. Companies that buy information from consumer panels would do well to obtain data from their information providers that allow them to construct this basic decision matrix.

Each box in the matrix represents a specific behavioural situation and is therefore analysed separately. Firstly, the number of consumers in each box should be established, then described in terms of per capita brand consumption, total category consumption, reasons for consumption, distribution channels used and preferred formats and packaging. This analysis provides an understanding of the quantitative significance of the crucial segment in the bottom right-hand corner of the matrix: those customers who are not only heavy buyers but also demonstrate a very high selection rate – fanatics, in a sense! They may only constitute around 20 per cent of the total number of consumers, but can account for 70 per cent of volume.

Most significantly, the matrix enables us to select target segments in which to increase volume, and to introduce marketing plans for each segment. We need to start by identifying the reasons prompting customers to consume little or not enough of the brand, as well as possible strategies for increasing this volume, even among the heavy consumers. Should we direct our efforts horizontally (by increasing the rate of selection) or vertically (by increasing consumption at a constant selection rate)?

Situational marketing

Increasing consumption of a brand is about attempting to widen its base and area of use. The battle is not so much within the product category itself as with other categories. In the distant past, beer in France was consumed only in the north of the country, or as an accompaniment to *choucroute* (sauerkraut) – and yet brands have since been able to change it into today's thirst-quenching drink of choice for modern men and women from 10 in the morning to 10 at night. In order to catch up on France's lagging cola consumption, Coca-Cola set up situational marketing plans, the most notable of which stated the intention of making Coke the No. 1 drink to accompany daytime meals. This potential market was such an enormous one that it occupied the majority of the Coca-Cola company's efforts. The brand has attempted to change French cultural habits by persuading them to substitute its own fizzy, sugary drink for their habitual choice of natural, spring or mineral water, and wine. It also faces competition from beer in this market. This calls for micromarketing work: defining a specific marketing mix for each individual consumption situation in which an increase in market share is planned. This volume-based work must therefore be built on a number of simultaneous situational marketing plans. Fine-tuned marketing of this kind rejects the illusory approach of tackling every problem with one big global campaign and promotional strategy. What are the main tools in this kind of situational marketing?

- *The first tool is targeting*. As any analysis of panels and megadatabases will show, the biggest potential for growth is generally to be found among the heaviest consumers of the brand or category; 20 per cent of buyers of Danone products account for 70 per cent of its volume and profitability. However, there is nothing to say that our biggest clients consume our product exclusively. There is always a potential for an increase in their selection score in existing consumption situations: it remains to analyse the factors holding back the growth of this selection score (image of the product, image of its use, format, packaging, tastes, distribution availability, price, etc). It is also possible to create new situations, increasing opportunities for consumption.

- A growth in volume often requires the launch of a specific new product or line extension. All impediments to consumption need to be removed. The impediment can sometimes be the product itself. For example, the beer giant Miller launched Miller Lite in the United States because it was easier to drink in large quantities than the standard product. Some readers will remember Georges Killian's *bière rousse* – the famous 'gentleman brewer' brand. It is less well known that the taste and texture of this beer made it practically impossible to drink two bottles consecutively: the product's composition thus gave the brand a structural handicap in terms of intensive growth. The same is true of Perrier, with its large bubbles, which are certainly distinctive but hinder repeated consumption, unlike the essential oils in Coca-Cola which make the drinker thirsty even after drinking. Coca-Cola observed that above a certain age, the desire to restrict sugar and caffeine intake was a subconscious impediment to consumption. This led to the creation of two extensions: Diet Coke and caffeine-free Coke.

  The recent French launch of Les Givrés d'Orangina (Orangina Frost) is an attempt to bring the brand's image closer to the ideas of thirst and extreme ice-cold refreshment. These concepts had previously been largely absent from the brand's positioning, which had concentrated on its exclusive high natural orange pulp content, making it virtually a liquid foodstuff. It is therefore significant that Les Givrés is sold only in one-litre bottles. Sensory analysis is another way of calculating the product's filling characteristics in fine detail. Orangina Red was launched to increase the consumption of Orangina among teenagers, who are the largest soft drink-consuming group. The formulation of Orangina Red allowed larger quantities to be consumed by particularly thirsty drinkers.
- The third factor in creating per capita volume is distribution. For example, selling the product in close proximity to the place of consumption makes the brand a virtually automatic choice. The Coca-Cola company works constantly to bring its products closer to the place of consumption. Automatic Coca-Cola vending machines can now be found in the corridors of every business school, airport waiting lounge, railway station, leisure centre, football stadium, swimming pool, etc. Taking the fixed

price at automatic machines into account, it also becomes possible to sell the soft drink at a per litre price higher than the equivalent price had the drink been bought in a one-and-a-half-litre bottle in a discount store. The proliferation of small outdoor refrigerators at bars and cafés serves no other purpose than this. Furthermore, it acts as a remarkable barrier to entry for all competing soft drinks: the café-owner will probably avoid putting cans of Pepsi or Virgin Cola in the refrigerator next to the red-and-white Coca-Cola colours.

Distribution is also the key to new situations of consumption that need to be conquered to widen the position of the brand. Considering the steady growth in the restaurant market, we can see that whoever controls the restaurants controls volume. It was not until 1997 that McDonald's in France began selling Orangina. Given the close link between teenagers and fast-food outlets – in terms of both image and volume – it is easy to appreciate the previous handicap facing Orangina without a presence in these temples of consumption, shaping as they do the dietary rituals and practices which are carried over into the home. We have all seen mini-posters in traditional cafés and newsagents advertising a fixed promotional price for a sandwich and a half-litre bottle of Coke. Here, an old consumption habit (in this case, of the legendary cheese and tomato kind) is being supplemented with a new one.

- *As the previous example shows, packaging must be adapted if we are to be successful in volume per capita marketing*. There is a world of difference between the 25-cl, 33-cl and 50-cl bottles. For hypermarket purchases, studies show that the shift from the one-litre bottle to the one-and-a-half-litre bottle produced an increase in net volume. Each format and packaging type should be adapted to its intended specific consumption situation. In other words, the important thing is to offer not a range of products but a series of targeted uses.
- *Price is also a key marketing tool in per capita volume*. This is not merely a question of lowering prices: anyone can increase volume by giving a product away. Many brands have slashed their prices only to sacrifice profitability and brand equity. This also calls for rigorous analysis and experimentation. In an attempt to combat the expensive image of its product and to

increase per capita consumption, Disneyland Paris conducted a painstaking audit of all of its prices. For example, it found that a starter for 8 euros and a main meal for 11 euros in a theme park restaurant were considered by visitors to be expensive, and they bought only the main meal as a result. Experimentation revealed that lowering the price of the starter and main meal slightly had the effect of persuading visitors to buy both!

- *We cannot generate new usage unless we give consumers reasons why the brand is perfectly suited to the new situation in question.* In the volume approach to marketing, volume must be divided into two components: the 'already won' segment and the 'still to win' segment. Each of these components needs investment. In the first case, we should always protect existing sales volume by supporting our current consumer base. This calls for an intangible budget which – thankfully – works on the basis of a diminishing investment per person: the longer an individual has been a consumer, the less needs to be spent. This is how loyalty produces profitability (Reichheld, 1996).

  Increasing volume through the conquest of new consumption situations (perhaps even within the target group mentioned above) also requires investment, but this time on a more significant scale. It is pointless to create a new market without a budget sufficient to achieve the goal of widening the brand's field of competition. It is not enough merely to make the right product available in the right format in the right place: you need to provide the consumer with reasons to buy it. Sadly, many line extensions aimed at widening the consumer base have been stifled at birth by a lack of communications support: it is not enough merely to add the product as an afterthought at the end of your existing commercials.

A textbook example: the mobile telephone market

Since deregulation of the mobile telephone market, operators have changed their strategies in favour of systematic price reductions to attract customers – an approach which makes sense only if the goal is actually to effect a dramatic increase in the per capita consumption of these same clients. The process of acquiring clients and winning their loyalty in order to generate exponential growth in their consumption offers the possibility of profits large enough to recoup the spectacular investment required in this market: in the recent takeovers of telephone companies, the valuation was directly proportional to the number of their clients on the basis of 10,000 euros per client! We will now consider some tools for generating per capita volume in this sector.

The first such tool is the supply of the product hardware (the handset) at a cost unrelated to its actual value. In France, unlike other European countries, the device is almost entirely subsidized and is included in the overall price of a fixed-cost package. However, once the phone is in the consumer's pocket, it starts to be used.

Because mobile telephony has its roots in the professional sector, operators have been forced to invent new, easy-to-use products with features targeted at the individual consumer. The French embodiment of such a device is the Ola, which could be considered as the (fixed-price) Twingo or iMac of its market. Ola is an ultra-simplified package created by France Télécom, based on the simplest mobile phone available. This makes it an ideal choice for consumers who are apprehensive of the mobile phone choice and usage and its multitude of options, tariff structures, hardware choices and variations. Recognizing that volume would increase as barriers were removed, France Télécom created and dominated the cardphone sector with its Mobicarte product, which promised an end to fixed charges and institutional ties. Paradoxically, users of non-fixed-charge mobile phones are charged a premium for this freedom: they pay more for their calls than fixed-charge subscribers do.

Bouygues Télécom, a newcomer, was the first company to appreciate the strategic value of the FMCG sector and a hypermarket presence. These outlets, in addition to popularizing consumption, contributed to the image of consumption without restrictions. The sale of communications at wholesale price to these outlets make it possible to sell on to clients at a discount price, further promoting the image of a restriction-free phone solution at an ever-decreasing price.

Services are another discreet yet highly effective tool for influencing per capita volume. The possibility of reduced-price calls to a selected group of our closest friends like the 'friends and family' package results in a significant rise in the number of calls made: communication is the new oxygen among the modern tribes. Constant and collective connection to our social network forms the basis of modern existence. The 'Call Waiting' option on an engaged line also increases consumption. While temporarily breaking off a conversation to take an incoming call, the user is charged for the extra time spent on this interruption, and subsequently calls the caller back. In the same way, the undoubtedly useful service of voice mail works on the same principle as the answering machine, which doubles consumption: callers who leave messages later receive return calls. Mobile phone recharging kits also play a subtle role in increasing consumption: experience shows that telephones with these kits are never out of battery power and can therefore make more and longer calls. As we have seen, the volume approach covers all aspects of marketing and requires constant, painstaking work.

Consumption and penetration

By targeting per capita consumption, it becomes possible to achieve a significant improvement in brand profitability at any given market penetration rate. However, as demonstrated by the work of the British researcher A Ehrenberg (Ehrenberg, 1972), market penetration and per capita volume are correlated. The leading market brands therefore enjoy not only greater penetration than the others, but also greater loyalty and higher per capita volume consumption. Ehrenberg called this phenomenon 'double jeopardy' (as seen from the challenger brands' point of view, of course). This suggests that the continued growth in brand loyalty and per capita volume will eventually result in an extension of the consumer base. We will return to this point later (see page 173).

fifteen

Rebuilding the lost relationship

Never before has there been such a preoccupation with forming relationships with consumers and creating genuine, durable bonds with them. Is this an admission of marketing failure? After all, surely the essence of marketing is a focus on listening to consumers to meet their needs more closely, and doing everything possible to produce satisfaction and loyalty… Given the plethora of books over the past few years on the subject of relationship marketing, it would appear that this is not the case.

In fact, the concept of relationship can have several different meanings, depending on the author. Some use it as the new name for loyalty programmes. Others understand it to mean a radically different management philosophy. All, however, seek to regain control of the lost relationship with the customer which the distribution sector now appears to regard as its own exclusive property.

Going beyond sales

Construed under the first of its above meanings, the approach sets out to replace immediate sales focus with the creation of a long-term relationship. This relationship is to be durable and personalized, and therefore more profitable than the never-ending pursuit of new prospects. Taking the scenario of a customer walking into a car showroom, this means recognizing the fact that if the customer is there, he or she has already chosen – or at least seriously considered – your brand from a shortlist of eligible brands. You must therefore do everything in your power to ensure that the customer wants to come back when next planning a purchase. How can you leave a lasting impression which will make your brand an automatic contender in four or five years' time? This approach is a radical departure from the philosophy of selling as many options as possible to the client during the first purchase.

The studies conducted by Bain Consultants have gone a long way towards diffusing the latter preoccupation (Reichheld, 1996). The compelling figures showing the profitability of loyal customers are now well known.

The most spectacular example of a successful loyalty strategy is Saturn, the car brand created by General Motors to undertake what was at the time (1980) an impossible mission: to produce an all-American brand and cars that would command better customer satisfaction levels and loyalty than brands and cars from Japan. Apart from a revolutionary dedication to product quality, this challenge took the form of a complete upheaval in the fields of 'sales', after-sales and ongoing follow-up (Lenz, 1999). Saturn replaced the transaction with the relationship. One of the key factors in its success was the effective way in which it implemented every aspect of the following principle: 'Treat your customers the same way you would wish to be treated yourself!' This oft-repeated statement has such major implications for the day-to-day operation of most companies that it generally remains a hollow phrase. It affects not only the 'sales' process but also the organization itself. After all, what does an average customer want, if not a single contact who can be reached at any time? This removes the distinctions between marketing, pre-sales and after-sales, and may even result in the creation of a single, unified customer database in place of the old system of one per company department or operation.

Another secret of Saturn's success was the creation of a personal touch in relationships. What does a 'relationship' ultimately mean if your contact is anonymous or never the same person twice? Saturn customers collecting their vehicle after a repair find a note from the mechanic who performed the work, giving his or her name and mobile telephone contact details for more information. Neither Mercedes nor BMW has yet offered a similar service. Their best efforts have been to send each customer branded magazines and regular promotional material covering a number of chosen topics. Unfortunately, service is not one of them.

Creating a personalized relationship is crucial, for this is how loyalty is built among insurance or bank customers, regardless of how many mergers and acquisitions come and go. On a personal note, I remember once receiving some promotional material inviting me to open a Banque Directe account, the French equivalent of First Direct. Curiously, the letter was signed by the marketing manager. This was a major error, considering that the whole point of a direct bank is its symbolically direct access to the banker – hence its description as 'private banking'.

A relationship-based consumer contract

The recent advent of mega-databases has now made it possible to deal individually and directly with consumers by respecting their uniqueness as individuals and buyers. This technological revolution has come at the right time for all brands facing the need to bypass the barrier of mega-retailers who prohibit any direct link with consumers. Companies are now able to identify their best clients individually – even when they number several million – and the tailored information held on each of them enables the right information or promotional offer to be sent at the right time. This does away with the negative connotations associated with traditional direct mass-marketing promotions. The database is therefore a tool for building an intimate relationship with your best customers to increase loyalty, to persuade them to try out new products, to keep them informed and to share the benefits of your brand with them. Lastly, the database promotes the sort of communication between the brand and its customers which goes well beyond the scope of customer magazines. As can be seen, this approach is at worst an attempt to make a positive improvement to the usual direct marketing and loyalty programmes, and at best the creation of a genuine bond of understanding between the brand and its best customers, based not only on an appropriate product range, creating customer satisfaction, but also on a set of shared values. The self-service brand rediscovers its lost proximity to its customers, both in the strictly physical sense and – where possible – in the psychological sense too.

It is a simple statement of fact to say that in any given market, the brand which enjoys the closest proximity to the client has a considerable competitive advantage; and this is the strength of the hypermarket chains. Major brands cannot satisfy themselves with being restricted to transient advertising campaigns and the limitations of shelf space. How are relationships to be built under these conditions? How can the brand communicate its values if it obeys the law of USP, which limits to short statements what can be said in advertising? Friendship is born of an identity of opinions, values, aspirations, and conceptions of life. Brands simply lacked the media to communicate these values. Mega-databases are, in theory, a powerful response to this problem. It is therefore not surprising that major groups have all concluded that the considerable investment this implies has been a worthwhile one.

In France, 60 per cent of Danone's consumption is generated by 6 million households, each spending in excess of 500 euros per year on the group's products. It is essential to know these consumers; to understand them; to share the values of each brand with them – this is how a relationship-based consumer contract is created. Annual investments of between 20 million and 30 million euros on potential customers are now apparently considered normal by the large consumer goods groups. After all, this represents an investment of between 30 to 50 euros per major consumer household per year! The immediate return can be measured through the increase in the selection score of already-purchased brands (up to a ceiling of 70 per cent) and in tryout rates for brands which have not previously been consumed. The advantage of large multi-brand groups is their ability to use this type of collective campaign to manipulate the two key leverages of brand sales: increased loyalty and penetration. This clarifies the role of the *Danoé* consumer magazine: to rebuild the link by nurturing loyalty and increasing the volumes consumed by customers who are already major Danone consumers.

There are some very positive effects to the use of this instrument: each brand is forced to define its source of inspiration, its values, and so on. A consumer contract which is founded on a relationship cannot be maintained by promotional coupons and special offers alone.

So are smaller companies and brands excluded from these new relationship-based media by prohibitive costs which can be made profitable only through a vast multi-brand portfolio? The only solution, other than relying on external databases, is to search for partner companies in an area of common interest. For example, Nestlé brings together a number of its brands around the common theme of breakfast, which is a strategic development area for the company.

Doing it together

The third meaning of relationship-based marketing covers anything the brand does in direct partnership with its clients. This is the meaning proposed by S Rapp and L Collins in their 'Maxi-Marketing' series (Rapp and Collins, 1994). The typical example is the annual gathering of Harley-Davidson owners at a location somewhere in the United States, offering the opportunity to meet and socialize with members of the company – who have also turned up to the event on their own Harleys!

The key concept behind this approach is that of 'doing it together'. Customer involvement is all the more meaningful where there is participation in a joint activity which becomes an emotional, intense occasion because it is centred around an object that is itself ego-involving. Other examples of this approach can be found closer to home: baby-changing points dotted along motorways during holiday periods are one way for baby-changing product brands to demonstrate their commitment to customer service. The 'Open Miles' operation run by the Hollywood chewing-gum company made it possible for more than 40,000 young people between the ages of 15 and 25 to travel in 'Greyhound'-style buses, thus cementing the brand's values of liberty, *joie de vivre*, escapism and travel. Chewing-gum itself may not be all that exciting, but the values embraced by Hollywood are. Here, the masterstroke was that the concept was not limited to a simple advertising campaign, but actually put to widespread use in a way that was meaningful to young people.

Forget the customer and think of the person. The Pernod-Ricard group, now the world's second largest spirit company, was a pioneer of this form of relationship marketing. Paul Ricard, the company's founder, used to tell his troops: 'Make one new friend every day.' Six hundred brand ambassadors (salesmen) multiplied by 365 days works out at a minimum of 219,000 new friends every year. The brand has created a strong bond through the actual presence and participation of its representatives in all social gathering-places such as bars and at events which symbolize friendship, celebration and a shared enjoyment of life – from *pétanque* tournaments to the famous Ricard Live Music events (free rock concerts). Ricard has become the brand of mass celebration, shared festive experience and happiness. This alone has been sufficient to maintain the brand's market share: despite retailers' own-brand copies and half-price *pastis* competitors, Ricard remains far and away the leader. Also, whenever the group buys a brand on the downturn, such as Larios in Spain, it often begins by cutting advertising expenditure and reinvesting in building a relationship with a group of new customers, who may initially be few in number but are nonetheless highly involved. Can you name any religion which did not start with a small group of zealous converts?

The Internet opportunity

The Internet has brought its own unique touch and power to the ideal of the brand relationship. More than just a virtual 'shop window' or a direct sales channel, it should be used as a tangible demonstration of the brand's new direction. It is a new area of excellence which the brand can use to create relationships. Establishing an Internet presence can, however, expose the company to unflattering comparisons if it is not done with proper preparation; on the other hand, simply ignoring this new sphere is effectively an admission of failure.

The concept of the ideal relationship is not about a Web site's aesthetic appeal or the skilful arrangement of its text and pictures. In brief, the Internet should provide a genuine service to the customer. Nivea's Web site should provide skincare advice for babies of various ages. Likewise, Air France should make it possible to monitor the progress of every flight, supplying precise information on estimated time of arrival, gate number and terminal. 'Frequent flier' clients with a collection of points to trade in should be able to select and book the flights on which they intend to use their free tickets; this would replace the current system, which is more akin to an obstacle course. The Internet is a unique opportunity to show the customer how hard the brand is working to ensure his or her satisfaction:

- working to save the customer time (a visit to a travel agency will demonstrate that this is still an extremely weak point for the airlines);
- recognizing the customer personally – not by name, but according to a personalized profile of interests and values, making it possible to offer a tailored, individual service;
- making everything 'as easy as possible' for the customer.

The Internet also raises the possibility of a different type of relationship: it enables virtual meetings between followers of the religion. It is the brand's responsibility to use discussion forums to encourage interaction between devotees and potential customers with an interest in the brand. This facility is, of course, also provided by the special pages set aside for this purpose in customer magazines; but the Internet makes such communication far more powerful, more immediate and less 'in the pocket' of the brand itself, giving it an interactive directness.

The Internet will do so much to change our expectations and behaviour that it is worth asking whether advertising as we know it (by which we mean traditional, unidirectional, non-interactive advertising) will continue to exist in the future. A number of brands are starting to pursue this new direction. The features which are now being supplied by TPS (a satellite television company) to its 800,000 subscribers, via a truly interactive terminal, are set to become the rule. All the major television hardware manufacturers expect to cease production of non-interactive sets in the near future. Procter & Gamble has just conducted a series of interactive advertising tests.

Brands' holy places

Retailers each have their own location – the store – in which to promote the value of their own brand. A relationship is created when this space ceases to be merely a merchandising outlet and instead becomes a place where a passion is shared. Virgin Megastore and the French Fnac multi-media store have both achieved this status. Customers stroll around, listen to the latest music, flick through the cartoon strips and buy refreshments, with no sales pressure. The Décathlon sports shop has gone beyond the store concept to create places where young people can go to express themselves, trying out products or enjoying their favourite hobby. It is hardly surprising that young people no longer refer to 'Décathlon' but instead to 'Décat': the abbreviation is evidence of a genuine close relationship.

Nike's aim in creating the amazing stores that bear its name was to create not a chain of direct-sales outlets, but an interactive environment which was 110 per cent Nike. Before being bought out by Adidas, Salomon had opened its first Salomon Station, located at the heart of a winter sports resort. The purpose of this store was to revive and strengthen the relationship between the brand and new generations of snowboarders, a group which the brand had initially overlooked to some extent. The main purpose of Salomon Station was to listen: young people came in, bought soft drinks, watched videos, browsed the Internet, asked questions and gave their opinions. It was a genuinely interactive venture. This type of operation is very different from the 'shrines' maintained by prestigious brands such as the châteaux of Bordeaux, the top Champagne houses, or indeed Roquefort Société's carefully organized cellar visits. As a rule, spirit brands do need some kind of 'original place' where the religion was first born. These are places where the divine is almost tangible, and the visitor feels within reach of the mystery of the sublime creation itself: the majesty of Veuve Clicquot in its cellars; Jameson, the great Irish whiskey at the Jameson Heritage Centre; or Société, the historic brand which founded the legend of Roquefort, in the depths of its mountain caves.

In Nike Town or Salomon Station, the public experiences a full relationship with the brand. It is also a new role, but one to which they will in future aspire. It is the role of the 'consumer-participant'.

The age of the consumer-participant

When the founder of Burton, the worldwide cult snowboard brand, was asked about his customers, he replied that they practically felt they owned the brand. They expected a different type of relationship. They didn't want to 'have it done *for* them', according to the traditional marketing approach, but rather *with* them. Of course, this is not to suggest that snowboarders are typical of the majority of modern consumers. However, they do reflect an attitude which is sure to increase in the future. Habits are hard to break once formed.

Young snowboarders want to find out more and take an active role in creating and building the legend of the brand. This means, for instance, that they want to get to know the people behind the brand and interact with them. In this type of relationship, the concept of the 'back office' disappears: in fact, the back office becomes the front office instead. They are no longer satisfied with being mere consumers: they want to be co-producers and co-participants too (Boisdevesy, 1996).

Brand 'mega-places' such as Nike Town and Salomon Station serve precisely this purpose: listening, listening and listening again. The Internet is also an invaluable medium in this reversal of the seen and the unseen; the back office and the front office.

Affinity marketing

For decades, sociology has been showing us the key role played by grassroots support and positive rumours in the success of new products (Kapferer, 1991). One after another, the major brands – even those with the most apparently 'global' approach – have discovered the benefits of what we should call 'underground' or word-of-mouth marketing. If the brand is to acquire a body of devotees, it will need to conduct in-depth work starting with certain hyper-involved micro-groups, even though their reasons for involvement may vary from group to group – and in some cases, from country to country. The important thing is to identify the sources of affinity between these groups and the brand. Word of mouth is the medium of communication between interest groups. Furthermore, visitors to a Web site are attracted not by the fame of the brand, but rather by the fact that they know it contains information which will be of personal relevance to them. Word of mouth works because they will be sure to tell their Internet friends about Web sites they have visited. Whereas one person may be able to tell a dozen or so friends in the 'physical' world, the Internet makes it possible for that person to reach hundreds of others through forums and newsgroups. This is the essence of viral diffusion.

The importance of interest groups has also led a number of companies to name their brand's Web site not after the brand itself, but after the need or area of interest which the site addresses: for example, Pampers' Web site is called 'Total Baby Care', while Ariel's is 'Washright.com'.

Finding such an affinity is a necessity for challenger brands competing against a dominant leader. For example, Havana Club, the genuine Cuban rum, competes against the American giant Bacardi. It has invested in every area of consumer involvement and affinity: tourists visiting Cuba, cigar-smokers, lovers of Cuban cocktails, people with a nostalgia for Che Guevara, and even within the Communist Party... To help consumers produce their own Havana-style *mojito* at home, Havana Club has also recently launched a special co-branded product in conjunction with Moulinex: a mixer in Havana Club colours.

sixteen

Energize the value chain of your brand

The modern stakes of brand equity

Brand capital has never been such a popular subject as it is today. At a time when mergers and acquisitions are rife, brands and their portfolios remain a necessary haven of stability and value. This is also a time of fragmentation and 'virtualization' of the media world, and brands have a role to play in maintaining some traditional customer certainties. Lastly, this is a time of power in the distribution chain. It has become crucial to maintain the bonds of loyalty and customer involvement; hence the current emphasis on creating what is known as 'relationship' marketing.

Faced with a shifting climate in which traditional frameworks are being pushed aside, the brand remains a firm anchor and reference point – indeed, perhaps the only one left. This explains the importance of what we might term 'brand marketing'; in other words, organization and action stemming from the brand and its values rather than from specific techniques, as has been the case until now. New technologies and traditional methods of communication are all simply methods of applying synergy to, and working together to, promote the growth of brand capital. The brand must be the central driver of all communications.

At present, however, an analysis of the actual situation within companies reveals a strong imbalance between excessive internal research into the brand and its capital and what actually happens to this capital outside the company, where it is diluted by new constraints. In fact, brand capital is hyper-analysed and optimized in theory, but in practice the mishandling begins at the point where the brand leaves the company's sphere of control. Share-of-voice fragmentation, the rise of private labels and the power of the distributors, combined with a lack of control over growing 'networks of recommendation', all mean that the effects of strategic planning are diluted in the wider world.

The practical effect of this threat of chronic dilution is that it is no longer feasible to implement concepts which restrict strategy to advertising alone and employ 'below the line' tactics exclusively. Given that spending on the media (in its narrowest sense) now often accounts for less than 40 per cent of brand spending, we begin to appreciate the anachronism of traditional operating practices. Strategy should now apply to everything which may be described as the brand's value chain, from the moment it is launched by the company to the point at which it is consumed and loyalty is generated. The problem of dilution also raises the question of how to maintain energy outside the company as the distance between the brand and its progenitor increases.

Evidently, this is a situation calling for a new type of research and action. It is this objective which we will now address.

Rethinking theory

Is brand management possible without theory? No. The simple fact is that today, marketing directors are confused and are no longer sure which bandwagon to jump on. The past 20 years have, after all, seen the spread not only of new technological tools but in actual fact, behind these tools, a fundamental questioning of brand management's underlying principles.

While we used to think of brand promotion work in terms of the traditional AIDA model and its derivatives (attention, interest, desire, action; repeat action, loyalty), tools such as relationship databases, the CRM and now the Internet have questioned the validity of this model by replacing mass marketing or segment marketing with the one-to-one, individual-to-individual model made possible by recent technological developments.

Does this mean that we should abandon the models which have formed the basis of marketing for the last half-century? Should we give up mass advertising altogether? Or should we concentrate our efforts on loyalty-based marketing, relying on data mining and the customer relationship? Should we concentrate all our attention and efforts on the Internet alone? Or should we instead keep a cool head, considering the tendency of all groups of sellers to herald their own technologies as 'essential' in order to gain legitimacy and boost sales? Surely the phenomenon known as 'technopush' (the technological lobby) must be pushing us too far, endangering the equilibrium of our brands?

It is fair to say that advertisers have to some extent been held to ransom; or, at the very least, have been the victims of structural changes within agencies. These agencies have become ultra-specialized (promotion, operations marketing, loyalty, PR, database management, web agencies, etc), and have therefore tended towards vertical solutions. However, from the customer's point of view, a brand can be defined as total accumulated experience, and is modelled as the sum of all points of contact with the customer. We can appreciate to what extent this tendency towards vertical supply has jeopardized integration in the coherent environment which the brand represents. While we would be wrong to oppose these techniques – after all, each of them forms a point of contact in its own way –we must still appreciate the crucial importance of making them work together.

The limitations of the classic communication model

The traditional marketing approach to brand management distinguished a series of key stages leading from recognition to knowledge, involvement, preference, purchase and repeat purchase. One thing is certain: this traditional model now faces a number of major implementation difficulties.

In this model, the power of the advertising budget represented the initial 'big bang' whose shockwave energized customers, distribution networks and the internal structure of vendor companies.

The purpose of this advertising was to involve customers, either on a rational or an emotive level, and to feed an image values system. Impulse and involvement thus both came from upstream, carried downstream by product pushes and in-store promotions.

The proliferation of television channels and stations, the time spent on the Internet by consumers and a general tendency towards 'channel-surfing' have produced considerable fragmentation within this initial shockwave. In practical terms, this has meant a decline in energy from upstream, which has in turn led to a deficient level of involvement not only among the (less well-mobilized) group of consumers, but also among distributors.

At the same time, distributors are becoming increasingly independent and resisting definition as 'mere' distributors, instead developing their own goals and strategies which are finding a positive outlet through the energetic promotion of their own brands and customer relations programmes. In only a few months, for example, Rik et Rok (a distributor's brand of children's products) has succeeded in accumulating a database of over 190,000 mothers attracted by the brand's vision and products.

Taking this situation into account, the loyalty theory has now convinced many marketers to shift downstream to keep their customers. This strategy entails first understanding customers and then acknowledging their importance in order to serve them better and thus provide greater satisfaction – a philosophy which accounts for the current proliferation of relationship- and loyalty-based marketing tools.

Recently, however, doubts have been expressed. Firstly, statistical studies show that penetration and loyalty are correlated: the major brands enjoy both high penetration and high loyalty. In other words, we ignore 'conquest marketing' at our peril. Secondly, in a world increasingly dominated by the Internet, the more virtual the goods and services on offer, the greater the need to re-emphasize tangible and sensory aspects, which are necessary catalysts for generating involvement. Lastly, aren't CRM techniques generating more of a calculated loyalty than a true consumer commitment?

Therefore, instead of setting up these strategies in opposition to one another, isn't it time we combined them? We shall examine a possible framework for such a strategy below.

How is value built today?

Integration always starts with the customer. What are the sources of value for a customer today? There are four: product, service, information and an affinity with the brand's core values.

In a world in which media pressure portrays the Internet as the apotheosis of all evolutionary development, and building relationships as the ultimate aim of traditional marketing strategies, we appear to have forgotten that the product itself is still a source of value. Every day, consumers continue to embrace new products and fall in love with the latest model of car, mobile phone or ready-made meal. Service also continues to play a part in influencing market share: it can be seen in the competition between airlines, banks, insurance brokers, telephone companies and online traders.

The Internet has revealed the power of information as a source of value, and it is true that this medium has at last given us access to free, effortless and personalized information. When looking for information about cars, features, prices and the best deals, 60 per cent of Americans now use the Internet, although a mere 2 per cent actually buy via this medium. Not to have an Internet presence is to miss out on the second stage of the AIDA approach by failing to answer the questions generated by this interest.

Lastly, the loyalty to which all brands aspire transcends mere calculation. Apart from the satisfaction provided by quality goods and services, genuine loyalty is an emotive bond strengthened by a shared affinity, outlook and system of values between the brand and the customer.

The value chain of a brand

How are the above values transmitted to the customer? Through the value chain, a series of links interwoven by a combination of:

- media advertising
- the Internet
- distributors

- opinion formers
- social communities and groups
- customers themselves

By combining the four sources of brand value with the links in this chain, which can be described using the analogy of a 'gas main' of brand values, we are faced with the question of how to breathe life into this model. Like a gas main, energy is injected along its entire length to maintain pressure. We therefore need to ask ourselves: have we primed the brand value promotion chain sufficiently well? Are there any 'leaks' in involvement anywhere along its length?

In the traditional marketing model, energy was injected from upstream through the power of the media, advertising investment and the impact of innovative commercials. We know that in reality, the fragmentation of the chains and of customer attention limits the model's effectiveness unless limitless budgets are available for media and GRP.

Today, energization is still the only solution – but this time downstream, at the very source of the brand – at the point of contact with the customer. Here, there is a rich potential seam of involvement to be mined. It is involvement of this kind which creates loyalty and lasting bonds.

Pathways to reinvolving the chain

Herbert Krugman, one of the great theorists in the field of consumer brand involvement, defined and measured this involvement in terms of the number of mental 'connections' which consumers made between their own lives and any given brand. Today, with this involvement dwindling as a result of environment pressure, we need to reverse this equation and build these connections ourselves wherever possible, a task which entails getting close to the everyday lives of our target groups and other players in the value chain. After all, what is a brand if not the sum total of its customers' individual experiences across the entire chain of communication? But what are the catalysts? When and how does this happen? To find the answer, we must look to the world of social science.

Reminder 1: Opinions are social

Mass-marketing models often overlook the fact that opinions are collective. In surveys and enquiries, consumers tend to speak in the first person and say, 'I like..., I think..., I feel...', but this does not mean we should believe them. Sociological data remind us that while opinions can be expressed in this way, they are actually formed collectively: each individual is part of an informal network of recommendation and has contacts with micro-opinion leaders. Individuals are de facto members of the brand's value chain and, along with distributors and vendors, must be energized and involved.

Reminder 2: Virtual, but also real, communities

We should recognize that the Internet has revealed the importance of communities, and therefore of 'common' factors based on shared values and interests. Virtual communities are places for sharing and freedom; they are spaces which promote the spread of interactivity. However, this statement needs a little qualification. The Internet consists only of virtual, and therefore remote, communities. The challenge facing the brand is not simply that of appealing to these communities alone. It must also energize actual communities which provide direct access to the consumer and can champion the brand once they themselves have been energized.

Reminder 3: Behaviour is the best predictor of behaviour

The Internet is a shrine to total interaction. However, this presupposes a willingness to interact in the first place. Customers must therefore be prepared to lay themselves open to the brand, its representatives and its communities. The 'one-to-one' approach is, by definition, selective. We must start by penetrating this filtering barrier, which we can achieve by obtaining permission.

The way to accelerate this process is to bring consumers into direct contact with the brand's values by involving them on a personal and behavioural level. Rather than just waiting for customer attitudes somehow to transform themselves into behaviour – the traditional marketing approach – we are reversing the order. We start by introducing energy in order to create behaviour, which has an additional advantage: behaviour always leaves a more durable impression on the memory. This is therefore a decisive step towards loyalty: after all, it is said that behaviour is the best way of predicting behaviour. Ideally, this behaviour should involve the consumer in a public sense, which is something the Internet cannot do.

Reminder 4: Only public commitment is enduring

It is one thing to engage in behavioural interaction (albeit to a limited degree) in public, but it is quite another to practise solitary interaction on the Internet. The psychology of involvement (or 'personal commitment') has long shown that opinions expressed in public, even insincerely, have a stabilizing and gravitational effect. It is as if public expression and action actually commit the consumer and become an integral part of his or her system of belief. This means that the best type of involvement is behavioural and collective involvement.

What conclusions can we draw at this stage?

Today, brands are no longer content merely to accumulate lists of contacts: their goal is to involve target groups. The theory of brand energization is focused on downstream factors; the target group's environment and expectations in every situation in which there is actual contact with the brand. This consists of creating lasting involvement by making a direct connection between the brand and the lives of the members of its target group, and by mobilizing all players in the value chain to transform them from spectators into actors.

Think communities!

As we have seen, if we are to create true affinity, preference and satisfaction, we must increase the brand's scope and effectiveness at each of its various points of contact with its target groups along the entire length of the value chain. After all, the closer the brand to its commercial intermediaries, opinion formers and consumers, the more effective it becomes. This leads to a new way of looking at the brand and its management.

All brands are community brands

Modern brands must now style themselves as community brands. After all, they rely on other parties to promote their products, services, information and values. It is true that the Internet, advertising campaigns and direct marketing can also achieve this effect to some extent: but they lack the essential component of emotive involvement. Furthermore, optimal involvement is created at points of contact with customers. We forget too easily that markets are first and foremost forms of dialogue which need to be fed, aroused, enlivened and energized.

Between mass-market advertising – always needed to create a collective image and shared awareness – on the one hand and one-to-one marketing – which is certainly personalized and interactive, but remains virtual and distant – on the other, the challenge facing a brand is simultaneously to mobilize and energize real and virtual communities, which both participate in the value chain, and to maintain a constant relationship with customers.

Stimulate conversations between communities

The Internet has revealed a hidden, and almost forgotten, dimension to the markets: they are forms of dialogue. This is a structural dimension which has vanished from the large hypermarkets, where anonymous customers hurriedly pushing trollies around the store rub shoulders but never talk to each other. Thanks to the Internet, the opportunity for dialogue between customers or communities now exists. However, looking beyond the exchange of information which this enables, we still need to create a long-lasting emotive involvement to energize the value chain.

Brand management's role in this process is to create and dynamize market meeting places where communities can interact publicly and thus become involved with end-clients, all under the aegis of the brand and its values.

Between mass marketing and one-to-one = one to few

Every new technique or technology seems to claim in its marketing that it renders all others obsolete, and therefore deserves the lion's share of brand investment. This rather excessively imperialist commercial attitude is very much in vogue at present: the 'technopush' of Internet providers has thus led to talk of a 'new economy', emphasizing the supposed obsolescence of other brand management tools. We must not let this distract us from our purpose.

The energization of the value chain always requires a collective pool of brand awareness and image. To consume a brand has often a badge meaning. However, this meaning must be widely recognized before the message can become decipherable. This is why we need a tool like advertising, which broadcasts this collective meaning: it is an irreplaceable catalyst for recognition and the creation of collective images. Costs have indeed risen as a consequence of the fragmentation of channels and the resulting 'channel-surfing', leading us to acknowledge the limitations of ever-increasing upstream investment.

Downstream one-to-one relationships presuppose a willingness to interact, but so many offers are being made by so many parties it is impossible to interact with every one of them. The basic requirement for one-to-one relationships is proximity marketing (or 'together marketing'), which seeks to activate the value chain by mobilizing participating communities of interest, especially by encouraging public interaction between these communities. The combined aim of mass marketing, segment marketing and one-to-one marketing must be to create and maintain collective involvement.

Implementation

For most brands, the mobilization of the value chain is a necessity. Brands such as these depend on a 'chain of recommendation' involving either formal (professional), informal or even virtual communities. It is impossible to move from mass marketing to one-to-one marketing without first taking the necessary step of energizing the chain.

The key concepts in this new awareness are proximity and commitment. The brand's values must be legitimized and promoted in places actually frequented by the consumer. Contact with the real world can only serve to improve the brand.

Implementation should be guided by four key principles:

- The brand's energy must be focused downstream at contact points with customers.
- Communities must become involved at a behavioural level.
- We must create public, inter-community commitment.
- We must therefore encourage, and even create, opportunities for 'dialogue' between communities and meeting environments in the chain of recommendation.

In practical terms, one needs to answer five key questions:

- Where downstream should we be focusing our energies?
- Which communities should we involve?
- How do we make the communities interact with one another? Where, and under what circumstances?
- Which sources of brand value should the interaction cover? Should it be the product, the service, the information or the brand's fundamental values?
- What are our objectives?

The intersection of our objectives (recognition, interest, action, loyalty) with the various links in the communication chain defines a strategic matrix. The same applies to the intersection between the sources of value in question and the links which need to be energized.

Link / Value	Company	Wholesalers	Retail distributors	Prescriptors	Communities
Product					
Service					
Information					
Core values					

Figure 16.1 Strategic Energization Matrix: Where to energize all along the value communication chain

seventeen

A new perspective on the brand portfolio

How many brands should a company keep in any given product category? This is the problem faced by most corporations today. The question forms the basis of all current studies conducted by companies whose business is moving to the international stage and thus to a form of total competition against other multinational companies as well as well-established local companies, low-price Asian imports and various distributor own-brands.

Large groups often make high-profile announcements on this subject; for example, Unilever announced its intention in September 1999 to scrap 1,000 of its brands and keep only 400. Shareholders and distribution are factors in what is undoubtedly a downward tendency. In the case of Unilever, let us remind ourselves that these 1,000 names represented just 8 per cent of the group's turnover. We can better appreciate the needless complexity and expense of supporting all these brands 'at any price'! The advantage of these headline announcements is that they give the whole company a precise direction and set timescales for action.

Brand portfolio optimization has strategic implications, for the chosen approach will have profound and long-lasting effects. Furthermore, brand reorganization affects a number of areas of the company in addition to marketing: production, finance and organization. It has strategic repercussions: the plan adopted may or may not lead to a long-lasting competitive advantage. Complexity is introduced whenever an attempt is made to provide a single, all-embracing answer applicable to all countries on all continents, as is now becoming the norm.

In fact, questions over the number of brands simply stem from the role of brand in the satisfaction of customer needs and the ability of the portfolio as a whole to provide more effective solutions to the requirements of the distribution channels than those provided by competitors. There are a number of factors which play an increasing role in this re-evaluation of brand portfolios: we shall examine each of them in turn.

In search of the mega-brand

A brand portfolio is a managerial response to specific targets established in an attempt to dominate a particular market, create entry barriers or win new customers and generate loyalty. Any research into this area needs to start by clearly establishing the objectives to be pursued and the precise expectations we have for our brand portfolio.

Nowadays, the main target is clearly one of market domination, which implies a need for the portfolio to be built around one ubiquitous mega-brand that will cement the company's distribution credentials. With its wide product coverage, it will have a strong customer presence in retail outlets, even if its products are dotted around the shelves (which calls for very strong brand identification symbols). The natural consequence of building a mega-brand is that brands which were previously important become downgraded. We need look no further for an example than the more limited role of the Plénitude, Progress, Elnett, etc brands in the latest advertising campaign for L'Oréal Paris'. The creation of a mega-brand will always have a significant impact on the balance between mother brand and daughter brands.

For this reason, portfolios which are too 'well balanced' would appear to demonstrate an intrinsic weakness: when innovation is shared between two brands of equal size, the impact of each is halved. This argument also applies to advertising: adding a joint sales force only serves to increase the handicap. The automobile industry is a case in point. The Volkswagen group has built its portfolio around the Volkswagen mega-brand. The PSA Peugeot-Citroën group owns two parallel brands of identical strength: fortunately, however, they are served by two separate distribution networks.

Making a mega-brand is difficult in the case of portfolios which have been very segmented, albeit for good reasons. Adidas is one such example. It bought out the Salomon group, which itself owned several highly specialized brands including the Taylor Made sports brand and Mavic (a producer of top-of-range racing wheels for bicycles). The brand policy of the Adidas-Salomon group is to maintain clearly delimited territories for its brands, each of which is intended to be the reference brand in its own sector. However, it was faced with the omnipresent and unique Nike 'swoosh' logo on every racetrack, court and green, demonstrating Nike's stated ambition of ruling the sporting sector. A division of brands of this kind was thus deemed counterproductive to the search for combined strengths which originally brought Adidas and Salomon together.

Why restrict this synergy to the back office? Although the implicit strategy was to maintain a portfolio of separate brands which were each to be leaders in their own fields, the ubiquitous 'swoosh' raised the problem of the comparatively lower profile of the Adidas logo. Surely one solution in such a case would have been to unify the logos of the two brands, telling the sports fan what distributors already knew? One of the great strengths of a logo is its ability to imply ownership without having to suppress names. However, the mere fact that these two companies have merged does not prove per se that there is any meaningful identity of values between football (the prototype at the heart of Adidas's identity) and new winter sports (snowboarding) (Salomon's target market). Furthermore, there is no reason to suppose that the distinction between the two brands in the shoe market will remain a clear one. If it does not, what image will we form of two brands with a shared logo in one single market? This demonstrates that choosing a multi-brand policy is a strategic decision which has far-reaching implications on visibility and critical size.

Think of the shelf!

What would happen if the Skali group were to dissolve one of its two brands of pastas (Lustucru and Rivoire et Carret) tomorrow? It would immediately lose some shelf space which its other brand would be unable to recover. Given the key role of prominent visibility in influencing purchases of self-service consumer goods – in other words, impulse purchasing (the main decision-making process used by consumers in this type of distribution) – it is understandable that manufacturers are reluctant to merge product ranges. In the short term, the risk of losing market share is a real one. Can it be offset by the potential gains in added value which this strategy can bring to consumers? Are there actually any such gains? Competing against the local market leader, Panzani and the new threat from Barilla, as well as the distributor brands, what would be the advantage in creating a third generalist brand? What, indeed, would be the competitive position of this third brand against the extraordinary popularity of Panzani (the leader) and Barilla (with its distinctively Italian image)?

The image of the strategic consultants recommending wide-ranging cuts in a client's portfolio of existing brands has become almost a caricature. This approach can overlook factors that are clearly based on empirical evidence and sound commercial sense, but which will continue to have severe implications for sales or, in any event, shelf presence for as long as distributors' own 'category management' is imperfect. In the toy industry, experience actually demonstrates that shelf managers purchase more if they visit several showrooms than if they visit just one. Promoting one single brand implies a tendency towards concentrating the entire product range into one single site; in other words, one single showroom. This means that the elimination of all minor brands in certain product categories results in a certain loss of potential revenue.

The distribution of roles

Experience proves that brand portfolios do not manage themselves: they need a coordinator who not only has a feel for each brand but also possesses the power to make decisions. Brands within a portfolio actually tend to be more preoccupied with their own relationship with each other than with the competitors they each face.

There are all too frequent internal battles over factors such as allocation of innovations, staff, ideas and resources.

Each brand should understand its own role in working towards and subsequently protecting the domination of its category, and should hold firmly to this role. For example, dominant brand leaders are frequently creating a negative attitude among a section of their potential customers. Some consumers refuse to buy the dominant brand, be it Michelin tyres, Levi jeans or Microsoft software, just as there are electricians who make a point of not buying products from Legrand, the undisputed leader in its sector with more than 60 per cent of market share. The reaction of this clan of refuseniks is directed more at the brand than the product itself. In this case, there is a need for a supporting brand which represents a genuine alternative to the leader brand. There are a number of very precise consequences to occupying this alter ego position in terms of products (identical), range (fairly deep and equally wide) and price. Brands of this kind need to give 'anti-leaders' positive reasons to buy in order to create a real brand commitment among buyers, and in this way make it difficult for new competitors to enter the market.

Once again, experience proves that managers find it difficult to stick to the role of the supporting brand, and often develop relative positioning strategies against the leader which fail to take account of the overall framework which has been built to defend a dominant position for the company.

First and second brands

The word 'second' should not be taken to mean 'secondary'; after all, the great films of our time have featured many fine supporting actors around the top star. 'Supporting' brands act like fuses, protecting the mega-brand or neutralizing external threats. The way in which the Coca-Cola company neutralized the threat from Crystal Pepsi by sacrificing its own Tab Clear is an example of such a role. (Zyman, 1999)

Crystal Pepsi was one of the most successful new product launches the United States has ever seen. One year later, it had become one of the most spectacular failures (although New Coke is certainly another contender for this crown). Crystal Pepsi – that is to say, a clear Pepsi (rather than the usual black colour) – was an attempt to capitalize on a perceived backlash against the cola category which had been driven by the appearance of so-called 'new age' drinks offering a healthier approach to the soft drinks market.

Crystal Pepsi's colour positioned it as a competitor to brands in the lemon or lime category such as 7-Up and Sprite. Coca-Cola then chose to launch its own transparent Tab Clear product, positioning it as a sugar-free 'diet' product. In doing so, it succeeded in persuading the entire market to associate the product's transparency with the benefits of the sugar-free category. The sole aim of this strategy was to kill off the new so-called 'transparent' (clear or crystal) category by confusing consumers' understanding and thus toppling Crystal Pepsi.

Indeed, consumers were unable to form an image either of how this category was supposed to taste (Tab and Crystal Pepsi had different tastes), or of how many calories the drinks should contain. Tab Clear boasted that it was calorie-free. Crystal Pepsi did not, and for one very good reason – it contained sugar. Crystal Pepsi was thus dragged into a category (diet drinks) in which it had a severe handicap: its sugar content. This new category was put to the sword by Tab Clear's intentionally suicidal strategy. To borrow the words of Sergio Zyman, who devised this plan for Coca-Cola, we need to distinguish between 'gorilla' and 'guerrilla' brands (Zyman, 1999).

What are the segmentation criteria?

Before we organize a brand portfolio, we must first answer the following question: what are the relevant segmentation criteria? Theoretically, there are many, for instance Bahlsen or Lu could divide their biscuit portfolio by product (sweet biscuits versus savoury biscuits), by price and quality, by use or conditions of use, by consumer benefit, by customer profile, and so on. The crucial question is therefore to decide which criterion or criteria to use in justifying the need for various brands. After all, it is one thing to tailor supply by restructuring a range, but it is another matter altogether to present that range as a number of separate brands. What tendencies can be observed here?

The higher the level of consumer involvement, the easier it becomes to supply a variety of brands. Higher involvement results in a narrowing of what consumers refer to as their ideal. This means that there are many ideals, and hence a proliferation of single malt whiskies, high-end luxury products and vintage wines. The distribution channels are also more exclusive, and media focus is more on word of mouth. Barriers to entry are based more on style and social factors than on economic considerations.

With a lower degree of involvement, the consumer tends to favour the big, universal, reassuring brands.

The concepts of 'general supplier' and 'specialist' also provide a firm base for a brand portfolio. Legrand is an international generalist brand in the light electrical goods sector. However, Legrand as a company also owns specialized brands – one per major product category.

In many cases, the distinction between a local brand and an international brand is a significant one. Local brands, as a result of their history, household market penetration and installed user bases, enjoy great brand equity based on reassurance, permanence and security. International brands may be seductive, but they also carry a higher price tag. However, we should remember that, if it wants to keep its status, the local mega-brand should also be nurtured by innovations, the same as the international brand, even if a judicious delay is necessary. The mega-brand should never remain behind current trends and fashions for long.

Dealing with the distribution channel

The distribution channels have become a major source of segmentation and reorganization of brand portfolios. The company has an obligation to provide an overall solution to the requirements of its main client: the distributor. For example, in the soft drinks or spirits market, the company must provide a complete portfolio of products, including well-known brands if possible. Some channels are open only to companies supplying a full range. This was the stumbling-block in the negotiations between the Coca-Cola company and the French government over the sale of Orangina. If the purchase had gone ahead, it would have meant the de facto elimination of Pepsi, the then partner of Orangina.

Channel-based specialization is becoming an essential strategy used by companies to segment their markets and organize their brand portfolios. This forms the basis of L'Oréal's strategy: Lancôme is dedicated to selective channels; La Roche Posay, Vichy and Biotherm specialize in pharmaceuticals or the foreign equivalents of the pharmaceuticals network; and the L'Oréal Paris, Maybelline and Laboratoires Garnier brands are targeted at the FMCG mass merchants. These last three brands also represent segmentation by consumer benefit and values. There is no particular reason why women across the world should choose to identify with the image of the Parisian woman. For this reason, the L'Oréal group bought the American Maybelline brand and now promotes it worldwide: its purpose is to promote the image of the American woman. For its own part, Laboratoires Garnier represents the expectation of a combination of a technical approach and natural beauty.

It can be misleading to attempt to judge the international situation from the rather unusual perspective of a single country's distribution system. For example, half of all bicycles sold in France are sold through large food-based hypermarkets. A further 30 per cent are sold in large specialist stores such as Intersport, Go Sport and Décathlon, with the remainder being handled by small independent retailers. In Scandinavia and Holland, however, where the bicycle is a daily method of transportation and is highly valued, the majority of sales are made by local outlets which are strong on service. Consumers in these countries expect to have a specialized repairer close at hand. How could these differences be reconciled in the future? If category killer Décathlon were to open more stores in Denmark, would it shift Nordic consumers' decision-making criteria away from local service and product quality?

For now, there is no one dominant distribution channel in these countries, but rather a number of different channels in competition with one another. Brands should take this basic fact into account. For example, in the United States it is impossible to sell a 'mass merchant'-distributed brand through assisted sales channels (such as department stores or specialist outlets). The Moulinex brand is sold through the former channel, while the latter is served by the Krups brand separate from Moulinex, although built by it.

This means that a company will have several types of brands in its portfolio:

- a mega-brand which soaks up most of the company's investment;
- brands aimed at controlling and dominating a distribution channel;
- specialized brands for specific market niches or slots (eg top-of-range);
- 'tactical' brands to take advantage of distribution opportunities without compromising the position of the mega-brand and the sales networks. This makes it possible to achieve market coverage through, for example, a presence in the mail-order sector, discounters and cash and carry firms and even on the Internet.

Internationalizing the portfolio

Internationalization raises the question of reproducibility of the factors of success. In their countries of origin, brands were developed gradually over time during a period when media costs were low. Conversely, brands expanding on to the international stage do so in an environment of competition and high advertising and distribution costs which bear no relation to those experienced during the company's growth in its own domestic market. In France, the Seb group comprises the Seb, Calor, Rowenta and Téfal brands, each of which has spent years building brand equity with its consumers. These names are ubiquitous in this sector's highly concentrated distribution.

Could this portfolio of brands be transplanted to Brazil and survive against local competitors, Korean and Chinese imports and international brands such as Philips, Black & Decker and Moulinex? Surely a different mindset and approach would be required. In fact, as is already the case in the United States, the key items in the range are available through the single T-Fal brand in the Carrefours and Wal-Marts of São Paolo.

The Vivendi group pursues the same branding policy in the services sector. In its home country, it is important for a group not to appear to be some sort of all-encompassing hydra or private monopoly: how would consumers react if they were to receive one bill from Vivendi for telephone usage, another for cable television, a third for water, a fourth for transport, and yet another for energy or waste disposal? This is why Vivendi has instead chosen to create a number of international master brands, each respectively associated with a different sector: Dalkia for energy, Onyx for waste disposal, Connex for transport and so on. However, would the same approach be necessary in the People's Republic of China? Or would it in fact be more advantageous to promote all these services there under the single Vivendi Environment banner?

eighteen

The realities of brand extension

No aspect of brand management is quite so hotly discussed as that of brand extension. This is hardly surprising, given that it is the most radical of the innovations offered by new-style brand management in cases where companies plan to capitalize value around one single name and create a mega-brand. Furthermore, two US authors (Trout and Rivkin, 1999) have made careers out of writing books and organizing conferences lambasting this practice, which they portray as a sure road to ruin via what they describe as an inevitable dilution of image. It is certainly true that not every brand extension is a success; but why condemn all of them out of hand? After all, there is an enormous failure rate among new product launches, but innovation remains the most essential of all necessities for a brand.

Extension is now an indispensable part of the life of a brand, for it represents growth, expansion of scope and market adaptability. What remains is to identify the right time, place and content for the extension, as well as the methods to be implemented for the launch. For example, Coca-Cola did not undertake its first brand extension (Diet Coke) until 1982, almost 100 years after the brand was first founded. Since then, brand extension has become a way of life for Coca-Cola, even though one such extension (New Coke) was such a spectacular failure that it has been described as the marketing blunder of the century (Hartley, 1998).

The case against brand extension

The anti-extension crusade is based on a nominalist understanding of brands, inherited from 'products as brands' policies in which a brand name indicated a single product, and vice versa. Ariel can be nothing but a washing powder; Sprite is simply a lemonade, and nothing else. Zealous advocates of this approach believe brand extension presents a confusing identity to consumers: the one-to-one link between brand and category disappears, allegedly damaging the brand. It is worth considering that this pessimistic analysis seems to have done nothing to harm Bic, which expanded from its position as a leader in the ballpoint pen market to become a world leader in disposable lighters, disposable razors and even windsurfing boards. Nor does it seem to have prejudiced the success of Virgin, which now markets a cola, an orange drink, a vodka, a British train network, a transatlantic airline, a chain of multimedia shops and a bank, etc. As to the Japanese, they seem to have been unaware of the concept of 'brand extension': it would never occur to them *not* to brand everything with the same name, that of their company, which for them is a symbol of intense pride. Mitsubishi has successfully branded cars, televisions, lifts, and so on ad infinitum. The same is true of Yamaha, a world leader in motorbikes but also in electric keyboards and classical pianos. Indeed, if one were to devise a phrase more likely to convey meaning to a Japanese audience, it might be 'brand secession' – the decision *not* to label all products with the umbrella brand name!

One thing is certain. Brand extension alters the relationship between brand and product, or indeed between brand and product category. Bic stands for pens and lighters and razors. Each of these Bic products has more in common with the others than just the Bic name: they share the essence of 'Bic-ness'; that is, an exclusive combination of several values (each product stands for good quality, good value and ease of use, and therefore is a natural part of a relaxed lifestyle). This combination of values has in each case captured a leading market share in each respective market. Since the brand has in fact created these segments, it has become the leader and de facto standard. If the combination were to have no resonance, the brand extension would fail: this was the fate of Bic perfume. However, new Bic tights seem destined for a glorious future in emerging markets and Eastern European countries.

It is not the intention to reproduce the content of the methodological chapter of my book *Strategic Brand Management*. Rather, after observing the realities of extension as it is practised by companies, a number of important points concerning the proper management of brand extensions can be made.

Bad reasons for extension

Extension is fashionable; perhaps even too fashionable. This is why many brands leap into extension programmes before they have exhausted all means of generating growth based on the core product. Extension rarely solves problems which stem from a lack of growth of this core product.

When La Vache Qui Rit (Laughing Cow) sales fell during the 1980s, the temptation for the company would have been to stake everything on extensions such as Apéricube and Toastinette to compensate for declining volume. Instead, the Bel group decided to rethink the entire marketing mix for the famous 'product with the round box' to get sales moving again. Such an approach overturned all previous taboos: nothing could now automatically be dismissed as impracticable or impossible, as is often the case when the problems being faced are relatively minor. For example, it was well known that the portions were fiddly to open: consumers always got a small amount of cheese on their fingers in the process. However, up until then, the cost of a new sealing machine had always been considered exorbitant. The rethink removed the validity of this objection.

Brand extension is a galvanizing force within a company, and one which often has a detrimental effect on the core product sales as the company pursues potential growth in sales which were weak to start with. For this reason, extension does not help to solve the core product's immediate problems, and may even indirectly serve to aggravate them by diverting resources away from the product: initially at an internal level, but often also externally, among consumers.

Thus it was that, despite the intense 1997 advertising for Orangina Red and its well-received advertising campaigns targeted at the teenage market, sales of the standard Orangina product continued to fall without being offset by increased sales of Orangina Red, Orangina Plus and Orangina Light. This is why the company finally decided to seize the bull by the horns and re-examine every aspect of the basic Orangina product's marketing mix in the light of one single question: how can we increase consumption? After all, what use is popularity if consumption does not follow suit?

When buying a brand, companies integrate into its financial value their hopes for future gains from extension into other (hopefully even more lucrative) markets, and then work tirelessly to vindicate the acquisition through a systematic policy of extension.

In this way Unilever paid a rumoured 100 million euros for the legendary Boursin, one of France's most famous cheeses, whose 'Du pain, du vin et du Boursin' (Bread, wine and Boursin) advertising baseline was the second most memorable of all French advertising slogans. Boursin enjoyed a spontaneous awareness of 41 per cent and an aided one of 90 per cent, and was No. 2 in the 'soft cheese with garlic and herbs' market behind Tartare (41 per cent compared to 31 per cent). There is no doubt that in buying Boursin, Unilever acquired a brand with a remarkable ability to open doors, leading the way for the addition of other cheeses to the range. However, the extremely high price paid by the group probably also reflected its desire to use Boursin as a way of penetrating the associated – and much larger – 'soft cheese' market (16,000 tonnes compared to 10,000 tonnes) which was dominated by Saint-Moret with 40 per cent of the market. These strategic aspirations, combined with a desire to achieve the necessary return on investment, explains why Unilever tried repeatedly to penetrate this market through Boursin brand extensions:

- The first attempt was the launch of the Nature Boursin plain soft cheese, which was only a limited success as Boursin's core image is its strong taste. A Boursin without this taste seemed inconceivable to consumers.
- Learning from this experience, the company decided on a complete repositioning exercise in 1994, this time targeting children.

The product was thus relaunched as Boursin pour Petits Gourmands ('Boursin: a tasty treat for hungry kids').

- When profits from this campaign were in turn judged unsatisfactory, the concept was simplified by relaunching the product under the independent Petit Gourmand name, which was unambiguously aimed at children – the Boursin brand name appeared small, only as an endorsement. Unfortunately, a lack of sufficient advertising support against the giants of the children's market (Petit Louis, Kiri and Samos) reduced this new product impact considerably. In 1997, the last three brands accounted for 92.4 per cent of the children's fresh products market, while Petit Gourmand held just 4 per cent.

There is too much of an implicit tendency to see extension as being mainly an opportunity to realize savings: there are optimistic hopes that the extension will succeed without requiring significant marketing and advertising support. This is a fallacy. One of the main causes for brand extension failures, as for the launch of any new product, is a lack of advertising support. It is pointless to try to enter a new market and do battle against well-established competitors in the hope of capturing a significant market share if the investment does not match the ambition.

When is an extension strategic?

What, then, are the 'right' reasons for extending?

The first reason is growth, but only after all other options involving the core product have been explored. Planta, a margarine brand, was created in 1959. In a traditionally butter-consuming country like France, it was originally positioned in the cooking and baking market. It was not until 1976 that the Planta Fin extension was first launched. The aim of this product was to penetrate the much larger 'spreadable' market by leveraging its new spreadability and improved taste, while capitalizing on the growing health awareness issues which were causing many consumers to turn away from butter. No other extension has since been introduced. Instead, a succession of repositioning campaigns and improvements to the mix have been introduced whenever sales have flagged to ensure the virtually uninterrupted growth of Planta Fin, even after the slump in the fashion for so-called 'light' products. This example is a good illustration of the main engine of extension: an opportunity to capture a growing segment by promoting the values associated with the brand which appear distinctively compelling in that segment.

Extensions can even have the effect of creating a previously non-existent segment. Amora's Tomatissimo product is one such case in point. In 1985, Amora captured the leadership of the French ketchup market from Heinz, the world leader (which had originally introduced the category to France). Amora's introduction of the 'squeezy' plastic bottle created a revolution in the way ketchup was used (packaging innovations can have a surprising effect on market share: Banga, the former market leader in still fruit drinks, lost its leadership once and for all when its rival, Oasis, became the first company to switch away from glass bottles!). In 1997 Amora, with a 47.3 per cent share of the market, set itself a goal of expanding the scope of the market by finding new consumers or new uses for the product. An examination of the barriers revealed that adults found tomato ketchup to be too sugary and hence too 'childish'.

Amora invented a new product for consumers who, although ketchup agnostics, liked tomatoes and tomato sauces. This was Tomatissimo, which combined the quality of an aromatic tomato-based sauce with a squeezable 'ketchup'-type bottle. The product was positioned on the 'condiments' shelves in stores, giving extra weight to the Amora brand's strong taste ('For the love of the taste') positioning. This extension, backed by two waves of TV commercials costing nearly 2 million euros, increased the brand's market share to 50 per cent in terms of value and caused volume to rise by 95 per cent with almost no cannibalization.

The second good reason for an extension is to increase profitability: this is not to be confused with reducing costs. Some markets are more profitable than others, either because of the cost of production, distribution or communication or differences in levels of price competition through the existence of distributor own-brands. The money to be made varies with the market: shower gel, deodorant and shampoo are not all equally profitable. If a brand's recognized advantages allow it to penetrate other growing markets with a more advantageous profit and cost structure, the extension is a desirable one. The reverse is naturally true: for example, it is doubtful whether Look, a specialist brand and high-end worldwide sector leader in the bicycle pedal market, would benefit from producing complete cycles under its own name, just as if Intel had launched its own branded computer. There is increasing price competition in the cycles market as a result of its domination by specialist distributors (such as Intersport, Décathlon and Go Sport) – a trend which is gradually extending across the whole of Europe.

The third strategic reason to pursue a systematic policy of extension is to maintain or increase the value of the brand in a constantly changing environment. Why did Nivea radically alter its worldwide brand policy – which had previously been focused on basic hygiene, concentrating on its flagship product (the little blue tub)? The most obvious explanation would be the change in the company's top management: the new team had a different vision of what was and was not taboo, or what was or was not desirable. Brand management, in fact, always stems from the decisions taken by the men and women at the head of the company. For as long as the company's founder remains at the helm, the brand's history and origins are ever-present in the collective imagination: this limits the scope for development of the product itself, which – internally at least – appears to be inextricably and exclusively, linked to the brand, and vice versa.

The main explanation concerns changes in the worldwide status of women. Nivea's German origins represented a particular era and feminine lifestyle which favoured the concept of skincare: there were no narcissistic preoccupations with beauty and seduction (unlike L'Oréal). Today, in the large, mature markets of Europe and the United States, the notion of beauty now has the upper hand. It would have been dangerous for Nivea to cocoon itself in a philosophy belonging to a different era, despite the fact that concerns of this type are now common once again, this time in developing Third World countries. This was the motivating factor behind a move from skincare to hygiene (deodorants), beauty (Nivea Beauty) and cosmetics. Also, margins in the lipstick and cosmetics markets are significantly higher.

Extension is particularly necessary for revitalizing long-standing brands or ageing local brands. A brand recaptures its market relevance, interest and up-to-date image by launching new products. However, we should recognize that in practice, there are considerable internal barriers to such extensions. Internally, there is too often a strong current of opinion in the sales force, marketing department or distribution section that the brand will not support such-and-such a new product. However, consumers themselves may be considerably more receptive to the idea.

The experiences of Kildamoes, the national Danish bicycle brand, provide a clear example of this misapprehension. This Danish market leader originally grew by focusing on everyday urban bicycles. Denmark is a flat country where everything is close together, making the bicycle an indispensable mode of transport. Kildamoes was shaken by the sudden arrival of a wave of colourful, high-tech off-road and mountain bikes from new brands which were Asian-produced but had distinctively American brands. The company's initial reaction was to launch an all-new brand into this market, believing that Kildamoes was considered too adult, too Danish, and perhaps even a little feminine. The consequent lack of success led management to relaunch these youth-oriented high-tech products under its own name through the usual sales channels. They were an immediate success.

We have too little faith in the power of local or long-standing brands. Only a few ingredients may be needed to revitalize them; most importantly, straightforward courage and enthusiasm, but also a dynamic and exciting product range. Had Kildamoes not attempted to ride the wave of popularity of these new sports, the brand could have become trapped in a permanent, outdated timewarp.

Budgetary errors

An examination of dozens of brand extensions reveals two common temptations – both fatal – when allocating advertising and sales promotion budgets for the extension launch.

The first of these has already been examined above, and consists of the belief that additional volume can be created in a competitive market without the need for investment. Miracles in marketing are few and far between. The principles which govern the success of new products invariably remain valid in the case of brand extension: shelf space, high profile, arousal of interest and product sales promotion are all necessary. This all requires a level of investment commensurate with the brand's ambitions. In many cases, budget discussions are held at the end of the development process and priorities often dictate that the extension will receive a much lower budget than had been planned.

The second error is to leave the central product exposed. All extensions are seen by the consumer as new propositions. Advertising presents the consumer with reasons to buy the new product instead of existing products in the market, our own included. If the extension is successful and the reasons to buy are attractive and persuasive, sales of our own products will be affected. Extension is not some sort of 'musical chairs' game: the aim is to expand the brand by widening its consumer base or its range of products and uses.

The example of Miller beer from the US illustrates this fact.

The United States has traditionally been a beer-drinking country. The management of Miller – one of the market's major beers, along with Budweiser, Heineken and Corona – observed that consumers seemed to have reached their limit after drinking two cans. Their response was to launch Miller Lite, whose stated promise ('Great taste, less filling') solved this problem. It was an immediate success. Unfortunately, the extension undermined their original product. They had forgotten to reinforce the reasons why US consumers should continue to drink the excellent Miller High Life beer, which had been their best-selling product.

Strategic extensions are attempts to effect a change in the market. You should therefore anticipate the effects of this change and take steps to ensure that the impact will be borne largely by your competitors.

A comparison of the respective budgetary strategies of Procter & Gamble and Unilever is most instructive. Procter & Gamble does not finance its new brands by siphoning resources from its existing brands: when it launched Pantène, it did not decrease its advertising campaign for Head & Shoulders. Before launching the Ariel Liquid extension, Procter & Gamble conducted an aggressive campaign in favour of the standard, powder-based product. In contrast, when launching Organics, Lever did too little to support Timotei.

Returning to the example of Boursin and its extensions, which we have examined above, the brand spent 15 million euros on advertising at launch time compared to Tartare's 10 million and Rondelé's 6 million. Boursin allocated 3.5 million of this total to the Nature brand extension, 8 million to the pepper-encrusted Boursin line extension and 3.5 million to 'standard' Boursin. It is obvious that Boursin led in overall share of voice. However, this masks the true story. The company had essentially funded its brand extensions by reducing the advertising budget for the standard product, which needed to be protected against Tartare and Rondelé, and still accounted for the majority of sales. When Lever launched its Axe extension (a masculine deodorant) in the after-shave products market (Axe System), the core deodorant's market share fell by 50 per cent. It was a risky gamble: if the extension failed to take off, the central product would be weakened without having gained any benefit from the extension. Sadly, this is exactly what happened.

Choosing where to extend

After culinary implements, where should the Moulinex brand go next? Which other markets could it extend into? Should it copy Téfal and move into the home protection and alarm systems market? Or should it leverage the skills of Mallory (its Brazilian subsidiary) to penetrate the ventilation market, followed by air conditioning? How do you choose a brand's new markets – its areas of extension?

The market should not only be fast-growing and profitable, but should also add value to some or all of the brand's attributes. This presupposes an understanding of the brand's core values; that is to say, the identifying attributes without which it would be a different brand altogether. These attributes may be tangible or intangible. Nestlé's Nesquik is about mixing chocolate with milk. Dove soap contains 25 per cent moisturizing cream, Taillefine is a 'weight-friendly' product, Danone promotes good health, Carrefour is serious and Marks & Spencer represents trustworthiness and attention to the needs of the consumer. These attributes could conceivably lead to the following extension markets:

- Nesquik: yogurts, cream desserts, sweets, cereals, bars, soft drinks etc, based on milk and chocolate;
- Dove: a deodorant which is ready to protect the skin;
- Taillefine: cream desserts and yogurts, but also 'snack' biscuits, and now mineral water;
- Danone: natural mineral water, *fromage frais*, cheese spreads;
- Carrefour: anything, provided the badge value or social image is not involved;
- Marks & Spencer: banking and financial services.

The overriding criterion is therefore one of the relevance of the brand's attributes in the market in question. We have already mentioned the failure of the launch of Axe System, a brand extension of the Axe deodorant, which was the European market leader with a 17 per cent market share. Axe System was targeted at the 'sensitive skin' shaving market. In fact, the qualities that made Axe successful in the deodorants market had no relevance in the extension market. Axe's deodorant is black, contains alcohol and has a strong scent: in essence, its success among 16-year-old boys was attributable mostly to the fact that it increased their confidence in themselves and their ability to attract girls. Only 1 per cent of men in the 18–25 age group claimed to suffer from sensitive skin – a figure which rose to 5 per cent among the over-35s. But what benefits did the Axe deodorant give this group? None at all.

In hindsight, we may ask why Axe System was ever launched at all. However, this would be to overlook the fact that in reality, the brand's underlying essence is not always immediately apparent. The importance of the seductive reassurance Axe gave self-conscious young men of that age was not understood at the outset. It was thought that Axe simply stood for 'men's deodorant', a purely marketing definition of the brand.

We should not forget that in marketing, understanding increases commensurately with action. It is simply not possible to possess total understanding before launching a product. Furthermore, the results of questionnaire-based studies are often ambiguous. A brand's strengths and limitations can only truly be understood in the light of active promotional work. Implementation teaches lessons no other pre-study would have revealed.

In the same way, Bic's failure in the leisure perfume market for young girls revealed the brand's limitations. Was there any other way of knowing this apart from trying? After all, brand history is full of apparently heretical extensions which succeeded: the Dim for men range, Vichy's Basic Homme, and Gillette's razors for women, for example. E-brands' management puts so much pressure on acting first that action does in fact precede reflection. There is hardly any time for prior research, pre-testing, etc. Only results will reveal some truths.

The example of Becel in Portugal is remarkable inasmuch as it demonstrates that it takes time and perseverance to identify those markets which are genuinely suited to brand extension.

Becel is a margarine brand which, because of its high polyunsaturated fat content and low salt and cholesterol levels, is thought to reduce the risk of cardiovascular disease. Despite this extremely narrow positioning and its unusual taste (it is salt-free), Becel is the second best-selling brand after Planta, and the best-selling hypermarket brand, as well as being highly profitable. It is a Unilever brand.

The brand was launched in 1970, and resisted all urges to extend for 15 years. It then began a systematic campaign of product launches in all markets in which it considered its positioning would give it an advantage over the competition: 1985 saw the launch of a Becel oil, while in 1988 it was the turn of a Becel mayonnaise, followed by a Becel cheese in 1990, a spreadable specialist Becel product in 1992 and a Becel milk substitute in 1993. Each one of these extensions was a failure, capturing less than 3% of market share. Fortunately, however, Becel margarine's market share had gone from strength to strength over this period.

It could be concluded from these unfortunate extensions that the company should have cancelled all other projects of this kind. However, it would have been a mistake to do so: companies should always be on the lookout for growth opportunities and more profitable categories. Becel's managers have gradually identified the highly specific factors valued by consumers among the distinctive characteristics of the Becel brand. They have learnt from experience that the mere fact that a product category contains less fat does not make it an automatic candidate for extension, despite seemingly favourable appearances.

Marketing is an experimental discipline. It is simply not possible to know all the parameters in advance.

How do we evaluate extensions?

When faced with a proposed extension, we need to start by considering its long-term logic. All extensions have an effect on the nature, scope and status of a brand. The first question to ask concerns the ultimate objective. An extension is like a staircase. Where will it lead to? What is our ultimate goal? In the final analysis, what do we hope to achieve with the brand? Considered in these terms, is the extension product in question a logical step along our chosen road?

The second question is this: what has the extension done to deserve the brand name? Does it possess the same physical or intangible characteristics – and if so, partially or completely? Therefore will the extension contribute to the brand's reputation on these attributes? Does it have other, additional benefits which will enrich the brand by lending it a dimension it previously lacked? When the Nestlé brand entered the refrigerated goods sector in competition against Danone and Yoplait, it acquired the image of freshness which had previously been lacking in a brand which specialized in dry products (powdered milk, concentrated milk, chocolate, etc) or frozen food. Experience shows that the real risk of dilution of brand image is high when there is no conceptual fit between the brand and the extension. Lack of physical fit per se is not that risky.

Internal relevance is one thing; the competitiveness of the extension product is another. As with any new product launch, we need to ask ourselves:

- Is the product demonstrably superior to the competition? If not, will the strength of its image be enough to make it appear superior or more attractive? This is the case for Nestea.
- Are there high costs and extended timescales involved in acquiring expertise in this new market? Will they result in too wide a price gap? This factor should never be underestimated.

When it moved from moisturizing cream to lipstick, Nivea had to learn a whole new set of management rules. Until then, the brand's stock-in-trade had been product ranges designed to last for years at a time. Players in the world of beauty products need to launch four collections per year! Entering new markets also involves adapting to a new shelf-buyer and distribution expectations. Could you do it? Would you do it?

- Is the target group for whom our consumer benefit is relevant, large enough in this market?
- Are we entering this market too late? How will our competitors react? Will we be able to fight back, and how? How will retailers view our entry?
- Will the extension possess the key factors for success in this particular market? Each market has its own rules. The extension faces a difficult task. It must retain the identity of a brand which was born elsewhere, in a different market, and was therefore nurtured according to the specific criteria for success in that market. At the same time, the brand will have to fit into the new market. If that brand is Nivea, is it possible to create an authentic Nivea advertisement which is also, and simultaneously, an authentic lipstick or deodorant advert?

Once again, this balance can only be found empirically, by trial and error, one stage at a time.

nineteen

Brands and the time challenge

In most companies, brand portfolios consist of some new brands and some longer-established – not to say older – brands. Although the latter are not generally renowned for eliciting passion from marketing departments and young managers, they still account for significant sales and profits in many cases.

Some very old brands always seem up-to-date, while other more recent brands already seem dated: compare, for example, Coca-Cola and Chevignon or Naf-Naf. How can we explain the difference between these brands? The problem resides in the balance between identity and change, and therein lies the brand paradox. How is it possible to build a brand – in other words, a precise point of reference – in an environment where everything, including competitors, distributors and consumers, is in a constant state of change?

The brand paradox

Fundamentally speaking, what is a brand if not a point of reference indicating one or more qualities and values?

To establish its status as a 'point of reference' or contract with the consumer, the brand must always remain constant in one respect: *for it to remain immovable some basic proposition of the brand is necessary*. When we talk of a brand as an intangible commodity, the word is well chosen, for it reminds us that the most important aspect to protect and keep intact over time is the intangible character of the brand. A brand which is unable to adapt its tangible characteristics

– in other words, its products – will quickly become obsolete. Brand extensions also show us that a brand created in one market can dominate others too: Bic's origins are in the ballpoint pen, but the name now also stands for disposable razors and lighters the world over. Bic produces many products, but its consumer contract remains intact: it produces everyday, easy-to-use items which make life simpler and represent good quality at a low price. This demonstrates that it is impossible to become a reference brand without maintaining a fixed set of principles and values over time, yet reshaping products constantly to satisfy consumers' ever-increasing demands for quality and service. Furthermore, new and more efficient market entrants are constantly setting new and higher standards of quality.

Brand identity can therefore only be created through a consistent consumer contract. At the same time, however, the market is changing constantly in every respect.

For example, emerging new lifestyles are often taken too lightly by the key market players, who later realize that they have 'missed the boat'. In the early 1990s, Rossignol and Salomon – two winter sports companies symbolizing competitiveness and the Olympic spirit – failed to realize that the bizarrely dressed bands of young snowboarders were the advance guard of a revolution in the entire winter sports industry. These young, laid-back 'fashion guerrillas' rejected the 50-year-old values and traditions espoused by these two brands in favour of Burton, Oxbow and Quicksilver – brands which might just as well have landed from another planet. Today, Rossignol and Salomon are unsure whether there will even be any 'traditional' skiers left in 20 years' time. Clearly, the problems affecting these two world-renowned (and once apparently invulnerable) brands are more than just a question of products: after all, they can make snowboards too. However, if they are to have any hope of remaining relevant, their whole system of values must change.

New distribution channels are sweeping traditional value chains aside as unknown leaders emerge from nowhere: companies such as Dell, Amazon and Yahoo! Each represents an entirely new culture (Slywotzky and Morrison, 1999). If today's female consumer, living well away from the major urban conurbations, can now buy cosmetic products from Nivea, Gemey, Maybelline and

Pond's in her local hypermarket, who needs the direct marketing approach of Yves Rocher, created to bring cosmetics to all women living too far from a specialized outlet?

Technology is also a destabilizing influence which can affect even multinational food brands. Nescafé has always promoted itself as an alternative to 'real' coffee for people who are either in a hurry or unsure of the correct preparation method. Nowadays, the latest range of coffee-makers from Moulinex and Krups are child's play to use, and produce top-quality coffee. What now is the rationale and relevance – in other words, the added value – of Nescafé? It is clear that the brand has reached its limit as a coffee substitute. Nescafé needs to become a mega-brand in its own right; intrinsically desirable, like Coca-Cola.

Changing to survive

Survival means change. This is the brand paradox. Some brands are like actors or singers: they stick doggedly to the same repertoire, to the delight of an enthusiastic but small group of fans who happen to like that particular style. Others are capable of surprising their audience by moving from one register and theme to another, acquiring added depth in the process and appealing to a different, wider audience; thus they gain an enduring appeal.

Brands which multiply entry points in their world will ensure their long-term survival.

The consumer enters the world of Calvin Klein via such brands as Obsession (passionate emotions), CK One (androgyny) and Eternity (idealized love). If Calvin Klein produced nothing but the occasional rehash of Obsession's 'torrid sexuality' theme, the brand would not have the same breadth. As it is, Calvin Klein stands for strongly expressed emotion: but not just one emotion. Each perfume is a renewal, and surprises a market which thought it had at last succeeded in pigeon-holing this heretical brand.

Range extensions make it possible to achieve this necessary mix of renewal and permanence, provided each of these extensions has its own individual character. Extensions of the La Vache Qui Rit cheese range are not merely variations of taste or texture: the goat cheese version adds a touch of impertinence, just as Orangina Red reveals a rebellious side to a brand 'approved of' by parents (and consequently less appealing to teenagers).

We therefore need to establish which aspects of the brand are inflexible and which others can be changed; put another way, what forms the essential core, and what is peripheral? By classifying too many aspects as inflexible, we effectively limit the brand's growth. Even the intangible aspect cannot remain inflexible, and therefore has to change. This often leads to painful, emotionally charged and frequently divisive changes: for example, luxury and rarity are no longer a core aspect of the Mercedes brand. It is attached to some products of the range (such as the S-Class) but not to others (eg the A-Class).

Determining a brand's core values

How can we identify which aspects of the brand could or should change without compromising its very soul? One answer to this question could be summed up by the phrase: 'Back to the Future'. If we understand the reasons for a brand's initial success and how it became elevated to the status of a brand in the first place, we will be able to recall the original equation. This is not a question of copying past successes by launching a 'new Beetle' or a 'new Mini'. We need to rediscover the essential components of the brand's consumer contract. For Mercedes, this means developing progressive cars; for Axe, it is about male seduction. The second stage is to consider the form this contract currently takes: in today's world, the 'macho seduction' approach used to launch Axe no longer works. Modern seduction is a more ambiguous matter, and now includes androgyny and bisexual overtones, among others.

Consumers also supply us with an insight into what constitutes the immutable character and central core of the brand. However, we should never forget that consumers have no long-term vision of the brand's own interest. The consumer's point of view should be considered in the decision-making process, but it is not a substitute for the decision itself.

Although qualitative studies assist our understanding of the core values of the brand, the theory of social representations provides the basis for the quantitative approach, which is vitally important – for strategic considerations are paramount. We need facts before we can make such risky decisions.

Image studies are not enough to establish the brand's core values. They are used to gauge the characteristics which are spontaneously associated with or attributed to the brand, yet there is no proof that these characteristics are indispensable in defining the brand; that is, if they were removed, the brand would be essentially different; a mere namesake.

The father of the core values concept was not a marketing expert. In 1948, Salomon Asch was a US university psychologist studying how impressions are formed. He observed that when a subject described a person, certain adjectives (such as 'cold' and 'warm') appeared to play a decisive role in creating the overall impression of that person. These adjectives, or characteristics, influenced the description of other characteristics used by the subjects to describe that person; their effect was in a sense a genetic, structural one.

We can extend this methodology for identifying core characteristics to brands. Instead of examining how a particular characteristic is associated with a brand, the key is to consider whether the absence of that characteristic would make such a profound difference to the brand that it would cease to be the same brand. We can discover the core values perceived by the consumer by adding this new type of question to our classical image or brand equity questionnaires.

Loyalty: the limitations of a mono-emphasis?

The greatest challenge facing a brand is how to continue to attract and seduce new consumers. At a time when the single marketing mantra is that of generating loyalty, retaining customers, life-long customer value and relationship-based marketing, this may seem heretical. Of course, we do need to nurture the loyalty of our best customers. All companies should obtain and act upon data on the

Brand	Market penetration	Rate of exclusive buyers	Volume per buyer
Maxwell	24%	20%	3.6
Sanka	21%	20%	3.3
Tasters Choice	22%	24%	2.8
High Point	22%	18%	2.6
Folgers	18%	13%	2.7
Nescafé	13%	15%	2.9
Brim	9%	17%	2.0
Maxim	6%	11%	2.6

Table 19.1 Link between market penetration and customer loyalty (*Source:* Ehrenberg, 1972)

increasing profitability of loyal clients over time; hence the perfectly sensible emphasis on customer satisfaction, special recognition for best customers, the pressing need to make use of data mining, relationship-based customer programmes, loyalty bonuses or schemes, customer support hotlines, etc – not to mention a host of after-sales tools...

Seen in this way, the pursuit of new customers (who generally 'start small' and often come to us from competitors), seems like a throwback to yesterday's marketing techniques. We are all familiar with statistical comparisons of the cost of acquiring a new client and the cost of keeping an existing one.

This emphasis on loyalty should not distract us from the fact that market penetration and customer loyalty are correlated. Incidentally, this is one of the advantages enjoyed by large brands: in increasing their market penetration, they simultaneously benefit from greater customer loyalty. The British researcher A Ehrenberg showed that the customer loyalty enjoyed by any given brand, like the average per capita consumption of that brand, was proportional to its degree of market penetration (Ehrenberg, 1972).

Consequently, it is difficult to generate increased loyalty in the long term without also increasing market penetration. The future of a brand thus depends on its ability to satisfy existing clients in order to increase their per capita consumption and selection rate, but also on its ongoing ability to attract new customers in order to increase its market penetration and in the meantime demonstrate its relevance to a changing world.

The problem is that the brand often means nothing to new customers, or at worst represents the past, making this target either an indifferent or an actively hostile one. Nonetheless, it must be conquered. This is particularly true of new generations.

The generation gap

Few variables have such a categorizing influence as age. Each age group has its own internal unity, shaped by the fact that all its members have been through the same historical events. The members of each group are linked by the common problems of life, work and love (making it possible, for example, to speak of the 'pre-AIDS' and 'post-AIDS' generations). Each group also resonates with its own pleasures, music, films, idols and preferred brands. As a result, a brand targeted at a fixed age-range needs to keep rediscovering and redemonstrating its relevance to its target group. The problem, as we have just seen, is that in many cases the brand means nothing to these people.

Consider the example of Damart, which specifically targets the older consumer, with its range of thermal underwear, comfortable ready to wear clothes and shoes. For the first time in human history, we will shortly be a society with two generations simultaneously in retirement. It will be increasingly common for a 58-year-old woman approaching retirement age to go shopping with or for her mother. Will she be happy to wear the same clothes and brands as her (older) mother? Is it possible to appeal to both generations at the same time? Men and women in their sixties are also keen to conceal the exterior appearance of their age: they want products which will meet their individual physical and psychological needs but are sold under 'neutral' brands whose image was sold to that age group while they were still in their forties. The paradox of all 'senior' brands, if they expect to retain an enduring appeal, is therefore that the products themselves must be 'senior' but their symbolism and consumer image must not. This explains the success of the specialized lines sold by large mail-order firms, or by such brands as Nivea or Pond's. By explicitly appealing to all ages, they have dispelled criticisms of a 'senior citizen' brand image.

Naf-Naf, with its famous 'little pig' logo, was – like Kookaï and Chevignon – a typical leisurewear brand of the 1980s, targeting the 18–25 market. However, the youth of 1999, having grown up with rap, NWA, *Pulp Fiction,* Obsession by Calvin Klein, Gap and Zara, have little in common with the youth of 1989. In this context, the brand's distinctive characteristic (the little pig) seemed to evoke a past era. The brand's continued association with this porcine caricature has immobilized it and provided a sign of its own mortality.

In a postmodern society, we increasingly inherit customs and values from our peers instead of our families. This has caused some brands to appear more distant and less relevant. For example, mothers used to teach their daughters to cook with Moulinex blenders and Seb pressure cookers. These brands thus inherited an emotive significance and familiarity which made them unassailable. Today, these practices have all but disappeared, weakening the relationship between brands such as Moulinex and Seb and their consumers. Even in the home they create less consumer involvement.

Consequently, the transmission of these transgenerational skills is now in the hands of the brands themselves. But the fact that 'your mother uses one' is a double-edged recommendation: each generation creates its own brands and identity. For example, the French *Télérama* TV guide owes its incredible popularity to its success in encapsulating the baby-boomer mentality with a system of values which has now fallen out of step with current trends in society. Reader loyalty for this magazine, whose name suggests television but whose pages are filled with other subjects such as art, culture, society, cinema, photography, opera and musicals, has never been stronger. Yet what does the future hold for *Télérama*? Will today's youth, more attuned to Virgin and musical Web sites, be reading it tomorrow? Should *Télérama* launch a brand extension targeting the youth market? Viewed in more general terms, this question reminds us of the need for a dual marketing approach.

The dual marketing approach

Too often, businesses ask the following question: should we work on promoting our relationship with existing customers, or instead invest in new prospects and new generations? This has become a meaningless question. The existing customer is an essential source of revenue today, so we must win his or her loyalty; but at the same time we must work on winning the potential clients of tomorrow. To paraphrase Collins and Porras in their book *Built to Last*, this is no longer a time for 'or', but for 'and' (Collins and Porras, 1994).

The forces arrayed against this dual marketing approach are many (Abell, 1993). Inside a company, it is common for the smallest difficulties experienced in targeting a new and younger audience to be blamed on the brand itself, as if it had no right to enter these new segments. This attitude generally has more to do with creating scapegoats than genuine analysis. Most often the problem is one of a product ill-suited to the new and disturbing demands of these new prospects. We can have such reverence for the existing product that we fail to prepare for the future. Yoplait demonstrated its understanding of modern values by launching its Zap product in Europe to appeal to a generation which had given up on spoons. Smirnoff was the first to realize that the recent crop of vodka converts are not keen on drinking from a glass: hence the creation of Smirnoff Mule, and now Smirnoff Ice, two original pre-mixed products which – like beer – can be drunk straight from the bottle in pubs. In addition, they match barmen's new expectations: it takes no time to prepare them and sell them, unlike a classic Bloody Mary.

Dual marketing also meets with another type of internal resistance: exclusive worship of the brand. In an attempt to appeal to the youth motorcycle market, which at the time had its ambitions set on the Vespa Typhoon and Booster models, Peugeot's marketing department first had to convince top management not to display the sole brand name in large letters, but instead to emphasize Hi-Power (the daughter brand), reducing the word 'Peugeot' to a smaller size. With the help of a 'graffiti'-style logo, a good product, a well-established network and a balanced dual branding, the product achieved unexpectedly high sales of 25,000 in 18 months. Peugeot had succeeded in making it exciting rather than conventional.

Sales forces sometimes contribute to company inertia. It is a fact that campaigns targeting the young generation in their chosen meeting-places are often in turn met with a cold, if not openly hostile, reaction: such scenarios are at odds with the positive relationships and feelings of mutual understanding which characterize salespeople usual dealings with familiar retailers. It took motivation and courage for Ricard's sales force to devise strategies for promoting their product among groups of business school and university students and in discos and themed bars already 'won over' to British and American drinks and Tex-Mex beers. Ten years on, the facts speak for themselves. Far from being perceived as a drink for an exotic older generation in the South of France, Ricard, the well-known aniseed apéritif, and the third best-selling spirit in the world, is taken seriously by people – including DJs – who frequent trend-setting venues across the whole of Europe. The brand was able to infuse these networks with its own values and form alliances such as the collaboration with the NRJ pop radio station over the Ricard Live Music concept, a series of free rock concerts which from 1988 to 1998 attracted a total audience of 3,900,000 young people. At the same time, it had recruited, trained, motivated and prepared a new, younger sales force capable of gaining proximity to the target group – in both the literal and the figurative sense.

Frequently cited are the dangers of alienating the brand's existing customers, who may disapprove of the very different tone used to attract the youth market. This risk is greatly overstated. In the case of Ricard, the distribution channels and retail outlets were watertight: the locales and events frequented by the 18–25 group were entirely different from those frequented by the older generation. The same is true for Smirnoff. For this reason, if *Télérama* were to seek to attract a younger readership, it would need to use the distribution channel of choice for young people – in other words, it should create a digital *Télérama* on the Internet, containing extensive coverage of all the available satellite or cable TV channels and targeted content, record reviews and clips, or film reports. There is little danger that traditional consumers of the paper-based magazine will ever sit down in front of their iMacs to browse the *Télérama* Web site, as many other publications have already demonstrated.

The Wall Street Journal keenly felt the need to attract a young audience which does not necessarily have the time to read an economics newspaper every day but still has an interest in economics and business, so it launched a digital version on the Internet. Its success lived up to expectations: 65 per cent of subscribers to the digital version were not already subscribers to the physical newspaper.

Faced with a similar problem of renewing its clientèle, the *Reader's Digest* decided to target young families (Seybold, 1998) by offering special Web-based themed issues with titles such as 'How To Protect Your Children From Drugs' and creating discussion forums around these themes. This long-standing brand took advantage of the Internet to build a community around relevant subjects and its own name.

A proactive strategy

Ricard's strategy was of interest because it was proactive. Anticipating a potential rise in the average age of its consumers, the brand took the initiative early on of making approaches to new customers. Most brands react too late, only when a close analysis of the data reveals that not enough new customers are being recruited while more and more is being sold to existing customers. The latter scenario calls for even more drastic changes.

Mercedes, for example, observed that its client base was getting older. Even owners of the smallest model – the C-class – had an average age of over 50. In an attempt to reverse this tendency and gain a foothold in the 35s–40s market, Mercedes sacrificed an image characteristic which had until then been inseparable from the brand itself: luxury. The brand worked to acquire three new attributes which it had been lacking in the eyes of the younger motorist: empathy, hedonism and solidarity. In practical terms, this has meant the launch of a highly diverse range far removed from the monolithic design which characterized all their vehicles so far. The company has thus unveiled a small runabout, a 4WD vehicle and a people carrier (the famous A-Class), all demonstrating that the brand is now listening to the market and new emerging lifestyles.

Other brands are branching out in order to adapt to this segmentation by age: Armani has created Emporio Armani, and Boss has launched Hugo.

Creating new prototypes

The Mercedes example demonstrates that if a brand is to rejuvenate itself, it must create new prototypes. Here, the concept of a 'prototype' does not refer to the technical notion of a pre-series model. It is based instead on one of the recent advances in cognitive psychology in the area of 'fuzzy' concepts. Indeed, modern brands are also starting to demonstrate fuzziness as their boundaries become harder to define and seem to have no limits: Danone used to be a yogurt, but it now manufactures biscuits for the export market and is launching a branded mineral water (as, indeed, is Nestlé).

At the heart of the image of these new fuzzy unities known as brands is the 'prototype'; that is to say, the product which encapsulates or carries this image. For example, when asked to define a game, people find it hard to offer a succinct definition. However, they are easily able to name a game which they consider to be typical. This is the prototype. In the same way, consumers find it hard to define what 'Nestlé is, but they have no difficulty in naming a 'typical' product (even though the name chosen varies from one individual to another). The prototype is the product which carries the image of the brand, as we saw earlier when we compared its image to that of the brand in general (see page 98).

Consequently, if we are to change the image of a brand, we need to create a new prototype. Given the difficulty of replacing one image with another in any given customer's mind, this new prototype will be easier to impress upon the memory of a new target group. In Mercedes' case, the goal of the A-Class is to become the new prototype for the brand, typifying its new characteristics to new target groups. As we have seen, product innovation is the essential key to rejuvenating the brand.

Core line and front line

Modern brand management therefore obliges us to avoid trapping ourselves in a monolithic concept of the heart of brand – its 'essence' and so-called intangible characteristics. Although it is necessary to establish a strong coherent identity over time using brand identity statements, the brand still needs the ability to surprise in order to remain exciting. This is the purpose of its 'front line' – unexpected bridgeheads whose purpose is to discourage too static a vision of what the brand is and what it is not.

For example, Michelin could launch a range of coloured tyres. In doing so, it would be rejecting the received wisdom that the 'serious' image of the brand and the product would be incompatible with a certain *joie de vivre*. The danger of a management tool such as the 'brand essence' is that it considers only the central core of the brand – while development of the brand takes place around its outer borders. Similarly, some products which are at first atypical later become the new prototypes of the brand, demonstrating its continuing relevance. Had it not made a foray into the world of glamour in the form of its lipstick products, would the Nivea brand have retained its relevance and attractiveness to the new European woman, even though its range continues to be based mainly on skincare products?

Bold promotional approaches

It is impossible to rejuvenate a brand without modifying its outward appearance and its advertising – especially when the intention is to send a clear signal to the market. Advertising exacerbates the problem of dual marketing: there is a fear that the act of wooing a new clientèle will scare away the customers who form the basis of existing trade. Experience shows that this is more of a problem to the companies than to the customers themselves. We should not forget that a brand should always project a favourable reflection of its clientèle; that is, the perception the brand forms about its own clients. For example, there is a perception that the typical Coca-Cola drinker is a young person. This is merely a reflection: Coca-Cola is actually drunk by all sections of society. Indeed, it is the most popular soft drink among senior citizens, a demographical group whose influence will continue to rise.

The purpose of advertising is always to create value among the clientèle: the brand is a source of added value. For this reason, existing brand customers participating in pre-test work for campaigns which are not aimed at them are far more open than we might expect. For them, the fact that their brand seems to be acquiring a cross-generational appeal is proof of its relevance and ability to escape the confines of the past. This adds value to their own self-concept and to their own image in the eyes of relevant others.

Repositioning: escaping the restrictions of the past

Over the life of a brand, declining sales bring with them a need for a sharp repositioning. The approach adopted in this case is radical: at no point during the search for possible new positioning strategies should it be stipulated that the brand must not distance itself from its former positioning or the brand's basic roots. Freed from this restriction, the cross-disciplinary working group will plough rich furrows of creativity, the results of which should be presented to consumers as part of an interactive process.

It should be pointed out that, on the contrary, when repositioning strategies are adopted to revive sharply declining sales, everything possible is done in general to preserve the core values and assets of the brand. As a result, the measures eventually adopted are uninspiring. Furthermore, the so-called 'assets' of a brand that is experiencing serious problems are probably not in fact assets at all. It would be preferable to give free rein to energy and creativity during the research phase, even to the point of allowing consumers themselves later to decide whether the proposed new strategy should be changed back to reflect more the brand's original identity.

part three

The actuality of brands

Every day brings fresh news in the domain of brand management. A merger between distributors perhaps, or a regrouping of manufacturers, or maybe a brand strategy in conflict with the received wisdom of the category. Through the lessons that they suggest, these events are the inspiration behind a commentary which appears regularly in such business or economic journals as *Figaro Economie* or *Les Echos* and *The Financial Times*. As new idea follows new idea, these events are quickly forgotten. Yet their lessons remain valid. It is for this reason that on the following pages you will find some of my most recent articles, which take the form of remarks on the actuality of brands.

twenty

Orangina: good value at one billion dollars?

Why was Coca-Cola prepared to pay a billion dollars for Orangina – nearly three times the brand's turnover? The answer is that a brand's financial value is an indication not of its past or present, but of its future growth potential. A brand's future depends on the ambitions of its owner and the resources that owner is prepared to invest to achieve them. Accordingly, Orangina is worth more to Coca-Cola than it is to Pepsi, which does not consider sparkling orange drinks to be a strategic product to add to its portfolio. For Coke, it would be a significant addition: the company would hold the world's No. 1 (Fanta) and No. 2 spots in the orange soft-drinks sector, each one with a distinctive positioning.

It is a little-known fact that apart from size, *there are many similarities between Orangina and Coca-Cola*:

Both are excellent products which appeal to local tastes in all countries where they are introduced. Both are also sold in distinctively shaped bottles distributed by bottling plants which are supplied with a mysterious and secret concentrate. This brand coveted by Coca-Cola produces good profits in France, where it is the market's No. 2 soft drink, and has a presence of one sort or another in 50 countries – from China to the United States – backed by a fixed marketing strategy: it is thus a typical example of a global brand. Above all, in acquiring the brand, Coca-Cola plans to remove the main structural restriction to Orangina's international growth: the lack of a good bottler. For the best bottling plants in many target countries – indeed, in many cases, the only bottling

Figaro Economie, 26 January 1998

plants – were already operated by Coca-Cola itself. This acquisition should also finally give Orangina access to mass-market restaurants and fast-food outlets the world over: after all, the growth of a soft drink depends on its ability to penetrate the food market by becoming a substitute for water. Other restrictions need to be removed, one of which is the price of the product. Unlike Coca-Cola or Fanta, Orangina's manufacturing cost is high – a result of the drink's 12 per cent citrus fruit content. The raw concentrate for Orangina is far more expensive than its Coca-Cola equivalent, and dilutes less well. This helps to explain why, as a 'natural' soft drink, Orangina is marketed abroad as a top-of-the-range product. Its market in the United States owes much to the fascination of young adults with so-called 'new age' drinks, promising to the health-conscious consumer a higher level of quality. There is therefore no danger that Orangina will divert sales away from Fanta (Coca-Cola's other orange soft-drink brand), whose 'youth' positioning will need to be reinforced.

Because Orangina enjoys only limited recognition abroad, its price will have to fall a little before sales will increase. This was not possible until now, as sales volumes were not sufficiently high to offset a price reduction. However, this will cease to be an issue if Coca-Cola buys Orangina.

Lastly, experience indicates that companies buying a brand have little of the previous owners' reticence. This was the case when Nestlé bought Perrier, and indeed when the Pernod-Ricard group bought Orangina from its founder. To reduce its cost price, it may first be necessary to demolish a number of former manufacturing taboos. Having understood all of these factors, we can begin to see why Orangina was worth a billion dollars to Coca-Cola.

twenty one

The future of Virgin Pulp

April 2000 witnessed the arrival of a new competitor in the orange carbonated soft-drinks sector: Virgin Pulp. After launching Virgin Cola to compete with the two giants, Coca-Cola and Pepsi, Richard Branson decided to turn his attention to Orangina. As one might expect, the launch was spectacular and unconventional: an open letter to the chairman of Orangina challenging him to an arm-wrestling match. But above and beyond this publicity stunt, will the new drink become a reality or is it merely 'pulp fiction'?

Paradoxically, Coca-Cola and Virgin are two of the companies with the highest cult image in the world. Virgin may even be the most extreme example of a brand with a wide diversity of product categories. It is not by chance that Virgin is represented by its founder and driving force, Richard Branson. Everything the company's chairman does embodies the brand and promotes its activities. But the durability of a brand isn't summed up by publicity stunts. In the case of soft drinks, it should be remembered that this is a heavy industry in which the key factors for success are advertising, distribution and price. Given that the Virgin Pulp product contains pulp, this already makes it more expensive to produce than Fanta. In spite of Richard Branson's high profile, it will also need to be advertised more extensively to appeal to young people outside the UK, where the Virgin brand is less well known.

In view of the need to have a distinct price advantage, in accordance with the brand's revolutionary programme (to free consumers from the giants, Coke and Pepsi), it is easy to see that this is a daring bid. The only condition of success is access to the widest possible distribution. Coca-Cola is easily available everywhere: there is not a single company canteen or restaurant, café or vending

Figaro Economie, 19 April 1999

machine that doesn't supply Coke or Diet Coke. In France, where Orangina also enjoys an extremely wide distribution, although less so than Coke, McDonald's has had to make an exception and add Orangina, in its characteristic little round bottle, to its menu. Virgin will certainly be available in shops, in trendy bars and in certain supermarkets where the distributor's brand is not particularly successful in the soft-drinks segment. However, Virgin Pulp will have to face the same harsh reality as Virgin Vodka, ie the absence of a sufficiently wide distribution. Why should mass retailers carry it? In short Virgin Pulp will probably encounter the same difficulties in France as Orangina does in other countries, in which case the result is a foregone conclusion.

twenty two

Coca-Cola or Micro-Soft Drink?

Scarcely had the crisis of June 1999 (concerns over the health aspect of cans) been forgotten and the volume of sales re-established, than Coca-Cola was faced with a new stumbling block, namely the French authorities' negative response to the purchase of Orangina. These two apparently unrelated events nevertheless highlight the fundamental distinction between the brand and the company, and the interaction between the two concepts.

The company is a collection of resources brought together around a particular economic aim. The brand is the name of a product or service which is different, superior and special. In the case of Coca-Cola, it can be said that the brand enjoys a fantastic level of popular support that makes it one of the strongest brands in the world, as is regularly evidenced by the publication of the financial values of well-known brands. However, the Coca-Cola company does not have an unblemished reputation. Although its financial reputation is indeed excellent – it is a basic value for any long-term brand portfolio – the company itself is arousing increasing suspicion and mistrust in Europe. How can you warm to a company whose former senior vice-chairman in charge of worldwide marketing, Sergio Zyman, stated that the company's aim was to encourage as many people as possible to drink as much Coca-Cola as possible at the highest possible price so that the company could make even more money? In his latest book, Sergio Zyman gives details of the strategies used by the company to 'neutralize' the competition. It is not my intention here to criticize what

Figaro Economie, 25 November 1999

is, after all, the inherent aims of any company, namely to eliminate its competitors. However, there is such a discrepancy between the seductive dialogue of the brand's advertisements, its omnipresent cultural, musical and sports sponsorship, and the brutal affirmation of the company's aims that one cannot help wondering whether this doesn't partly explain Coca-Cola's difficulties in Europe. For those who know it, the company seems to be the symbol of triumphant capitalism, advocating free competition, but is in fact doing everything within its power to eliminate that competition and subscribes to no other law than the one expressed above by its head of marketing. In fact the company's image weighed heavily in the authorities' decision to refuse to allow Orangina to be taken over by Coca-Cola. Furthermore, before there was any mention of a takeover, Orangina had instituted several proceedings against Coca-Cola for the abuse of its dominant market position – all of which promised to be successful. This merely confirms the reality of a company for whom the ideal of competition appears to be a total absence of competition. Rather like Microsoft. However, the company is remarkably well protected by its brand image, as evidenced by the latest crisis in Belgium. Heavy buyers soon returned to former levels of consumption because they have confidence in the brand and their experience of the thousands of bottles and cans drunk in the past without any ill-effects. However, once you leave the sphere of consumption and enter the realms of public administration, competition and market analysts, the brand image doesn't provide such good protection. Similarly, when it comes to influencers, medical authorities or even mothers, the company's ambiguous aims and biased behaviour tend to interfere with the advertising dialogue. In fact, the company's ideal would appear to be the disappearance of mineral water from consumers' tables. Under the guise of meeting 'consumer needs', this is a company which tries to change cultural habits but won't admit to what it is doing. As can be seen from the above, companies that try to be too dominant and impose themselves as the consumers' only choice will find that they have to contend with the resistance of the citizen and society in general.

twenty three

The distributor at the heart of the organization?

In senior management structures of FMCG groups everywhere, one question is being asked with more and more urgency: should we organize our sales forces – or even the organizational structure as a whole – around the customer; or in other words, the distributor itself? This is revolutionary thinking. After having structured our companies around products, and then around geographical areas (countries or regions) and categories or needs, we may now see dedicated sales forces and even whole management teams assigned to specific retailers, those whose weight justifies such a proposal. There are a number of factors which make this change inevitable.

- Considering that Décathlon, for instance, accounts for 30 per cent of Nike's sales in France (which is more than the brand's total sales in a number of other European countries), it would be impractical to maintain sales forces which target specific countries, actually accounting for fewer sales than this one retailer alone. As distribution becomes more and more concentrated – a process which is still far from reaching completion – 60 per cent of all Danone's sales in France will soon be made to just three major clients. These are figures which must not be ignored.
- There are already major account managers and large retailer coordinators in all corporate groups, but these are not 'line managers', and are assigned only limited power. Of course, this

Figaro Economie, 9 November 1998

applies even more at a European level. But as retailers themselves come to operate increasingly at a multinational level, it will be difficult to maintain local (ie national) sales and negotiation structures when faced with an international buyer who will seek terms based on consolidated sales.

- Finally, the single European currency will be a motivating factor in creating an organizational structure based on the distributor. The price transparency created by the euro will highlight unjustified price differentials between one country and another. These local differentials will endanger the brand's worldwide profitability if the distributor takes the lowest price charged as the basis for negotiation for the whole of Europe. It must therefore be possible, for example, to order a specific country's marketing division to increase the price of a brand, even at the expense of market share, in order to preserve the overall European balance for the brand.

As we can see, we need to replace the rather impotent 'key account' coordinator with one dedicated European sales manager for each distributor client. Trade marketing, which has until now been seen as a local, tactical operation, will come to assume its full significance once the client is established at the heart of the organization. And when we refer to 'the client', we are referring not to the end consumer, but to the initial buyer.

twenty four

The impact of the euro: 'squashed' prices

The recent economic crisis brought consumers into the age of hypersensitive prices. In the budget hotel industry (known as the 'no-star sector'), for example, studies have shown that consumers are sensitive to a price differential of one euro per night. Hamburger buyers base decisions on differences of ten cents. Producers and distributors, whether they like it or not, have had to adapt to this new order. And now, just as they have done so, the euro is set to effect a revolution which will sweep away all the old certainties.

After the 'low price' era, we are now entering the 'squashed price' era. For instance, in France, the division of all prices by a factor of 6.5 (the rate of the French franc against the euro) destroys consumers' psychological price barriers and, at the same time, distributors' pricing policies. Concepts of what is and is not expensive, good or bad value or a low or high price are essentially subjective. They are the result of a balance between quantity, quality and price. By dividing all prices by 6.5, the euro telescopes price differentials and makes promotional offers (which are known to account for up to 30 per cent of sales in some product ranges) look considerably less appealing. This has the effect of creating uncertainty over the future of such offers.

The euro will reduce the perceived price differentials between generic products and distributors' own brands as well as between these own brands and the leader brands, creating additional uncertainty over the growth of distributor brands which have not yet been able to build up customer loyalty.

Figaro Economie, 11 January 1999

Lastly, the euro will upset the old order of 'psychological' pricing. A price increase from FF 4,70 to FF 4,90 is not the same as an increase from FF 4,90 to FF 5,10. In the latter case, we have broken the five-franc barrier.

Euro currency equivalents for the above example would be 0.71, 0.74 and 0.77 respectively, affecting the second decimal point only. The FMCG sector has weaned us on a diet of 'low, low prices'. The euro destroys these differences and raises enormous questions concerning consumer behaviour. However, consumers are still left with the major brands, the 'hard discount' retailers, the seductively packaged premium goods and retailers' on-shelf recommendations. Who will win? There is as yet no answer to this question. Fortunately, many countries have opted for a period of transition, a term synonymous with 'training period'. Top management everywhere will be paying particularly close attention to future consumer panel data. However, the risk is that consumers will leave it until 'E-Day' before they pay in euros. In that case, there will not be time for market testing.

twenty five

Restoring consumer confidence

After years of untroubled calm, the realities of the food chain have recently been highlighted by a series of revelations, each more worrying than the last. Even more seriously, the discussions conducted under pressure between France and Great Britain on the lifting of the beef ban seem to flout the very principle of precaution in whose name the aforementioned ban was not maintained: the 'European' argument appears to carry more weight than the protection of individual Europeans. Whichever way you look at it, we are well and truly embroiled in a risk society. Where there was once unquestioning trust and confidence, there is now mistrust and even defiance. A society cannot exist without confidence in its key players. So how can this confidence be restored?

A number of recent food crises have highlighted risks that were hitherto unsuspected by the general public and only occasionally by specialists and even the authorities themselves. It is significant that the major fast-food chains had for a long time been changing their beef suppliers, and this was not merely to favour economic integration or to improve their public image. Similarly, as enquiry followed enquiry, it became obvious that the government departments concerned were more or less informed. However, through negligence, fear or a weakness in the system, the information was not passed on and *a fortiori* no preventive action taken. At the end of the chain, consumers were the last to be warned, and even then it was left to the crises to force the issue. It is obvious that, in future, consumers will have to be responsible for changing their own behaviour since the

Figaro Economie, 6 December 1999

authorities and organizations that were supposed to protect them have failed. Whether these are brands, government departments or the distribution network, consumers can no longer afford to delegate the management of their own risks. Hence they must be given the means to make informed choices.

According to the psychology of risk, it is a well-known fact that risk is overestimated by consumers when it is unknown, perceived as uncontrollable, or when they do not expose themselves to it voluntarily. The obvious example is the risk associated with the consumption of beef and the baffling rise of Kreutzfeld-Jacob disease. To this is added the more pernicious risk of the accumulation of infinitesimal amounts, believed to have a long-term effect. This proposition is often difficult to refute in scientific (what is meant by 'long-term'?) and especially psychological terms (it is extremely plausible at face value). Here again, refutation is a matter of confidence: who should we believe? These aspects of the psychology of risk in fact indicate the ways in which consumer confidence can be restored. The first is to reduce the dependency of consumers who, until recently, were 'pure consumers', ie they were reduced to the simple function of consumption. They must now decide for themselves whether to expose themselves voluntarily to risks or not. If they are to do this, however, it is vital to recreate transparency in the offering so that consumers know what they are buying. Hence the importance of informative labelling and especially labels of origin. Consumers have the right to know what they are buying so that they can take responsibility for making their own decisions. If they don't want to eat meat containing artificially high levels of hormones, then they should be able to make that choice. They should also be able to choose not eat French or British beef. This particular issue, however, raises a potential contradiction between the clause in the Treaty of Rome designed to suppress any form of discriminatory labelling, which would adversely affect the free movement of goods, and the basic right of all individuals to be free to control their own choices and risks.

Distributors, who by their very nature have close contact with consumers, were swift to respond to this demand for transparency, which is not only the right of all consumers but also a basic human right. Today, all distributors aim to guarantee the origin and traceability of their fresh produce. The retail business is based on a trust and confidence that is reinforced on a daily basis on the supermarket shelves and by the service offered to customers, who want to be able to make rapid choices with a guarantee of quality. To enable them to do this, they must be given clear and unequivocal information.

Modern society generates risks, through the knowledge brought by scientific advances and their promotion via the media. We are all confused and unprotected in the face of these potential risks and must therefore be able to rely on other players. We may dream of an administrative super-authority based on the US Food and Drug Administration model, but the companies and brands that are much more closely involved in our everyday lives can in fact be a more effective source of confidence due to their close contact with the general public. It is therefore important that they give a clear indication of the values on which they will never compromise.

twenty six

The Stock Exchange online: from company to brand

According to the latest figures for access to Internet sites, in May 2000 one of the most popular home-information sites was Boursorama.com. The site, which was accessed by 8.5 per cent of Internet users, ie 341,000 visitors (excluding return visits) who each consulted the site for an average of 43 minutes (Source: MMXI Europe). The fact that a stock-exchange site has proved far more popular than any of the other general information sites (ahead of dailies and weeklies) only serves to reinforce – if indeed there were any need to – the impact of the Internet in influencing the behaviour of private individuals vis-à-vis the Stock Exchange and, by extension, the companies quoted. But are the companies themselves really aware of this impact?

It is an understatement to say that the financial information provided by companies has acquired a strategic importance as a result of modern management's obsession with the creation of shareholder value. Today, this phenomenon is accentuated by greater concentration and the increasing number of mergers and acquisitions, and a new development whereby transactions are tending to favour the exchange of shares – ie purchasing powers – in preference to liquid assets and cash. This is why it has become crucial to maximize the price/earnings ratio (multiples) of shares and therefore continually increase the prospects of future profits. Depending on the development of these multiples, shareholders become either

Les Echos, 17 July 2000

prey or predator. A few months ago, Elf could have acquired Total, but time and circumstances decided otherwise. Total bought Elf.

Traditionally, a sound financial communication consisted of responding to the demand for information on multiples by the interested parties: specialized journalists, analysts, institutional investors, trustees, bankers and, finally, the general public. However, these various players did not share the same mental outlook and therefore did not have the same requirements with regard to information. For example, the general public tended to pursue long-term objectives vis-à-vis the Stock Exchange, which meant they were unaffected by short-term fluctuations and trends. The principles of financial communication remain the same but the Internet has deeply modified the mental outlook of the players, and even created new players to whom companies must now respond.

Surveys show that analysts, journalists and influencers – who operate in hyper-time and are required to respond rapidly and provide information immediately – are making increasing use of the Internet. However, the information provided on the Net is more susceptible to rumours and manipulation. In the past, when analysts, journalists and decision makers received a fax bearing the company stamp and brand logo, they had visual proof of its authenticity. This authenticity disappears in the anonymity of the messages sent via the Net. So how can these players authenticate information quickly and without losing too much time? And who takes the time to do this? Very few.

In this respect, the Internet 'disembodies' the company, makes it less tangible, less of a physically reality. However, at the same time, it makes the Stock Exchange accessible to a new category of private individuals known as 'day traders'. These are young Internet users, speculators in search of a short-term 'added value' rather than a long-term investment. They pick up on rumours and 'tip-offs'. They don't necessarily know about the company in question since, for them, it's not so much the reality of the company that matters as what is said about it, its present image and the predictions associated with its name.

This tendency to 'disembody' companies also applies to a third group of investors, ie those who are geographically removed but who are able, via the Internet, to invest when and where they want to, on all stock markets. For them, companies are not a physical reality but merely a name and / or a brand.

In the past, the reality of a company provided a wonderful buffer against the vagaries of the economic climate for local, individual or institutional investors. For example, because the French were familiar with Total as a physical entity and an industrial reality, and its network of gas stations had been part of their life for decades, they did not react particularly strongly to the *Erika* tanker disaster. In fact they were extremely tolerant and viewed it as a regrettable but temporary accident. But what does Total represent for international investors who are *a fortiori* likely to adopt a more ethical stance? A name, a title, a tarnished reputation that nothing offsets or redefines. The company is reduced to its simplest form of expression: its brand name, but without the emotional baggage of proximity, history, cultural involvement in national life and a familiarity that is reinforced on a daily basis.

It is therefore easy to understand why markets have become more volatile, with the new mental outlook and the new players created by the Internet making a major contribution. So how do we adapt to this new culture of brands and information?

First of all by being constantly on the alert, at all times, to what is being 'said' on the Internet. If something is said, anyone, anywhere in the world, may quite naturally want to verify it on the company's authentic site. Sites should therefore be regarded as continually evolving 'counter-sites', rather like the 'rumor-clinics', the columns in which the US daily press 'posted' a new rumour every day during World War II.

Second, by being aware of the importance of the psychological factors that influence the evaluation of brands. It is interesting that the English term 'goodwill' is used to define both the intangible financial asset and what creates that asset, ie the overall reputation associated with the company name. It is time for companies to take good care of their own brand name, their company brand name, since this is what counts in today's marketplace!

twenty seven

Luxury brands on the Internet

An e-luxury Web site was recently launched in the United States with a view to selling the products of the leading international luxury brands on line, including those of the luxury leader LVMH group which was actively involved in its creation. LVMH has in fact continued to operate at Internet level in the same way as at the so-called traditional level of physical distribution by taking over DFS, the leading duty-free operator in the South Pacific zone.

On the e-luxury site, brands will be presented in a sort of shop-within-a-shop. However, they will only sell part of their range: a selection of the most representative products as well as the new products most likely to appeal to a clientele of Internet users. It is now a well-known fact that the latter prefer to surf the Net rather than go shopping in the accepted sense of the term and therefore do not frequent the traditional outlets associated with the provision of services or the presentation of luxury goods. The e-luxury site will represent the essential 'running-in' and 'apprenticeship' stage that precedes the ultimate 'risk' phase, ie when the luxury brands will have their own Web sites selling their complete ranges direct and offering customized services. As far as the Internet is concerned, the approach can only be experimental since this is a new and continually evolving sphere in which action is the only way to learn and draw lessons before moving on to this ultimate and inevitable phase. However, luxury brands more than any other brand categories have a great deal to gain but also a great deal to fear from the Internet.

Figaro Economie, 10 April 2000

The leading luxury brands are characterized by their international reputation, an element of fantasy and desire but also by a fairly limited distribution which, by its very nature, introduces a rarity value which makes them even more desirable. Some of the consumers who dream of acquiring a particular brand are often either physically removed from the points of sale or daren't go into them for fear of not having the experience or self-confidence that is apparently required to frequent these intimidating sales outlets. In this respect, there is a fairly significant group of credit-worthy consumers who pose no threat with regard to the 'cannibalization' of the so-called 'bricks-and-mortar' distribution network.

However, the Internet will pose a completely different and crucial set of problems for luxury brands. In the first place, there is no luxury without a certain rarity value. It is significant that, one after the other, the leading luxury brands are moving from a reduction in the number of franchises, through selective and then exclusive distribution, to a fully controlled form of distribution managed by the brand itself. The Internet is in fact the complete reverse of rarity since it is accessible to everyone. It also offers the opportunity for pirate sites to sell discounted luxury items direct, by buying their supplies on the grey market. It is therefore crucial to resolve the paradox of an industry defending the legitimacy of selective distribution circuits (service will out!) within the context of EU legislation, while at the same time selling direct on the Internet via freely accessible sites. Furthermore, how do you justify allowing an e-luxury site to offer discounts on luxury items while refusing to allow Ashford.com to do the same?

The second challenge presented by these so-called 'pirate' sites selling direct on the Net is that of price. In fact, luxury could not exist without a disparity of prices at international level. For example, it is more expensive to sell luxury goods in Tokyo than in Paris since taxes vary considerably from country to country. These disparities explain the queues of Japanese tourists who increase consumer 'traffic' in the Parisian boutiques. For the Japanese, shopping for luxury items is one of the attractions and pleasures of a visit to the French capital. By contrast, for many people one of the main reasons for using the Internet is to find a bargain in a particular area. So how do you meet this new demand without destabilizing the balance of prices that has been patiently built up over the years between different countries and distribution networks? For the moment and in view of the risks, luxury brands don't want their sites to offer their products at discounted prices. However, at this stage, it is impossible to estimate the relative cost of returns or of the construction and management of the site. No doubt these figures will be closely examined by all the players involved in e-luxury with a view to establishing a new price balance in the very near future.

twenty eight

From Disneyland to Amazon.com: the harsh laws of economics!

There is a strong tendency on the part of the new – extremely promising and well-publicized – sectors that are being regularly created to encourage their many – small and large – potential shareholders to forget about the harsh laws of economics. In fact, everything is presented as if these sectors were opening up completely new perspectives, and even entering a new era, in a bid to demonstrate that classic points of reference and economic principles are now obsolete. In so doing, they relieve themselves of the obligation to prove that all this will be extremely profitable since the canons and dogmas of standard economics are no longer relevant. El Dorado – or rather the Stock Exchange – is within easy reach.

Almost ten years ago, Disneyland Paris was one of these new sectors, a fact which is all too readily forgotten. The European response to the American model is undoubtedly a great commercial success given the increasing number of visitors (over 12 million per year) who flock to the park and its hotels and are delighted with the experience. This makes 'word of mouth' and public rumour the park's best form of publicity. Unfortunately, it is still a financial disaster. The 23 or 24 billion francs invested will never be recuperated at the current prices, which explains the successive and inevitable moratoriums.

Figaro Economie, 4 September 2000

And yet one can still remember the certainty of Disney's senior management, who swept aside all objections and not only succeeded in getting the French political and administrative establishment to agree unflinchingly to the project, but also to provide a number of additional advantages, including a free TGV (high-speed train) line and the park's own station. The rest of the story is common knowledge.

Amazon.com, the creator of online commerce and symbol of the new economy, came into being just five years ago. With 20 million satisfied customers, it is the most high-profile representative of this new sector. Unfortunately, like Disneyland Paris before it, Amazon may be a brilliant idea but is so far a financial disaster. Even so, in the face of increasing criticism from Wall Street, its stock-market value is due to the confidence of its countless shareholders who, through the concept of 'new economy', have been led to believe in the miracle with just as much certainty as their predecessors. Amazon also has the support of an impressive media hype that has helped make the brand one of the stars of the Internet.

However, in spite of its commercial success, the real question behind Amazon and many other consumer-led Web sites is that of the cost of the service offered. As the symbol of online commerce, Amazon has to offer consumers the basic advantages they expect from e-commerce: a much better price (cutting out the middleman), a plentiful supply of unbiased information on products, and an ultra-personalized interactive service. By guaranteeing delivery dates, Amazon cannot delegate the service but must manage it, and its warehouses, directly. This creates major structural costs. Given the relatively low unit price of a book and the small profit margin, it is obvious that the balance and success of the system depends on growth, both in terms of the volume of buyers and the total number of purchases made by each buyer. The costs of permanent advertising are also high, with offline publicity the most costly item. The only solution is therefore the permanent extension of the offering, above and beyond books and CDs. Today, Amazon is offering consumers the opportunity to buy toys, tomorrow it will be cars. But this systematic wide brand-extension policy runs the risk of diluting the character and the identity of the company.

As can be seen from the above, new economy or not, companies come and go but the laws of economics remain the same. Disneyland Paris and Amazon are both brilliant ideas and their creators, visionary geniuses. But no company, whether real or virtual, can sustain losses indefinitely. As far as Disneyland Paris is concerned, the government and the Paris region are too heavily implicated for the park to close due to bankruptcy. One day, the investments that everyone knows are irretrievable will be 'written off'. However, if Amazon continues to make a loss, it won't be so lucky.

twenty nine

Is there room on the Internet for a 'brilliant challenger'?

The arrival of Amazon.com in the European online book and CD sales market was – hardly surprisingly – viewed with great interest by all players and observers in that market. However, behind the reassuring words of the firms with an existing market share in this sector, there was concern over the potentially fundamental difference between the structure of competition in the so-called 'traditional' economy and its equivalent in the new economy. The concern of these firms was not that Amazon would 'reshuffle the cards' or shares in a market in which, in any case, the new company and its much-trumpeted launch had been virtually instrumental in developing. Instead, the fear was that Amazon would eliminate the competition entirely, as often happens in many categories and areas on the Internet.

In the traditional economic model of inter-brand competition, there is often room alongside the leader for a strong challenger. Thus we have Coca-Cola and Pepsi, McDonald's and Quick in Europe, Avis and Hertz, Adecco and Manpower, among others. This is all as it should be. In the 'real world', four factors contribute to the emergence of strong challengers:

- The first factor is the distributor – the intermediary between manufacturers and consumers. Distributors hate being dependent upon one single dominant supplier, and will do anything

Les Echos, 30 October 2000

possible to generate competition by encouraging the challenger, creating a counterbalance.

- The second factor is based on differences in accessibility: proximity is, for example, a decisive factor when choosing a gas station or a fast-food restaurant. In this way, by occupying prime sites, Quick has been able to compete against the world giant that is McDonald's.
- The third is a reaction by consumers themselves against excesses of size: when a brand is seen to be consumed by everybody, this prompts an equal and opposite reaction among a large number of its clients. The same is, of course, also true for fashion: a brand worn by everyone is a contradiction of the desire to stand out. However, we can also observe this phenomenon at work in products with no 'fashion' status: there is, for example, a degree of anti-Michelin or anti-Microsoft sentiment among consumers.
- The fourth factor is that the groups into which customers are segmented are characterized by very different psychologies. You can't please all the people, all the time.

We should recognize that on the Internet, three of these factors favouring strong challengers simply disappear. The Internet is appealing precisely because it 'cuts out the middleman', rendering distributors' balancing acts and games null and void. Secondly, distance becomes irrelevant on the Internet: all brands are equally accessible. When a dot.com brand has a high Web hit rate and controls a large share of the market, the intangible characteristics of this brand and the low public profile of consumption go a long way towards counteracting the third factor mentioned above. This leaves only segmentation to give a rationale to the concurrent growth of two or more brands in the same market area or sector: the French Chapître.com, for example, which is fighting for market space against Amazon – the world's biggest online bookshop – specializes in rare and out-of-print books.

There are, however, several specific factors which encourage the creation of de facto monopolies on the Internet. For example, we need only take a cursory look at the structure of market share in the European online auction sector to observe that auction site Ibazar enjoys a dominant market position. Shopbot Kelkoo is on its way to doing the same in the sector of assisted purchasing and price comparisons. Internet-only brands have no physical presence, and therefore rely mainly on the mechanisms of the human memory and so-called spontaneous awareness. The first brand to establish its position in the collective consumer consciousness (for example, as a result of considerable offline publicity over time) creates a 'memory block' phenomenon which is one of the causes of the famous 'pioneer's advantage' in a market.

Secondly, the more customers visit a Web site, the more used they become to its layout: they find their way around easily, to say nothing of the interactive aspect which will allow the site to recognize them with a simple click of the mouse, increasing customer satisfaction through the speed and personalization which this feature offers.

Lastly, on the Internet, success breeds success. Like programs such as Word and Excel (which make inter-computer file transfer increasingly easier as their use becomes more and more widespread) an increase in the number of Web site hits produces benefits for users themselves: price information, inter-customer discussion or gossip, reassurance and advice flow more easily between customers on one single site.

If our hypothesis is a valid one, this implies that sectors containing several dot.com brands are inherently unstable and short term in nature: for any given product, the long-term distribution of market share should reveal a dominant and profitable leader as well as a number of less profitable challengers who have no alternative but to sell up. Risk capital companies should never forget this fact when choosing their investments.

thirty

The rise of licensing: when brands come before products

Brand management is experiencing a profound upheaval which may be as significant as the Internet in terms of the change it brings. This is the 'total dematerialization' revolution. Brands are acquiring the purely symbolic status of money, giving them a new and hitherto unknown potential for circulation and liquidity. More and more companies turn to licenses to create profitable brands. From this point onwards, the management strategy will consist of finding markets which lend substance to a valued name, in order that it may be turned to competitive advantage (and therefore profit). The most representative example of this new perspective on the brand is that of the rise of licences of all kinds (sports or media heroes…), and of Virgin, a brand equally capable of lending its name to soft drinks, transatlantic air travel and banking services. This is in sharp contrast with the traditional way brands were built.

From the product to the brand

Brands are not born, but instead developed over time. Of course, legally speaking, a brand exists from the time trademark is first registered. However, from an economic point of view, which focuses on the creation of value, the mere ownership of exclusive rights to the mark does not in itself create any value for the brand.

Le Temps Strategique, March/April 2001

In marketing, perception is everything. It therefore takes time for the brand name to acquire value and become sufficiently endowed with meaning to persuade buyers to pay more for products which bear the brand name. How exactly does this process work?

Every brand starts life as no more than a name on a product – or, more precisely, on a *new* product.

We could in fact define a brand as the name of a new product which has been successful – an achievement in itself. The key fact to remember is that, at the beginning of its life, a brand is virtually powerless. Unknown and imageless, it has no influence over buyers (other than, perhaps, the slight influence of a 'good-sounding' name).

The process begins with the product and its ability to promote its own superiority, either by demonstration or by reputation (the testimony of satisfied users). Nike was originally nothing more than a strange name: however, it represented a running shoe which was revolutionary for its time and worn by a number of US sprinters. This initial product played a founding role in two different respects:

- It paved the way to financial success – and therefore company growth – by enabling the production of other new products and providing access to media advertising, generating initial recognition for the name.
- It forged the long-term image of what the word Nike stands for. The psychology of perception reminds us that the meaning we assign to a concept is drawn from the first example we encounter which embodies that concept. As the popular phrase has it, 'first impressions are usually right' ...

The psychological term for the above example is the 'brand prototype'. We should not underestimate the importance of this concept (also referred to in terms of the 'flagship product'), which establishes its collective image. We shall return to this point later.

As the company grows, extending its distribution networks and acquiring the ability to invest in mass-media advertising, the brand name begins to attract not only greater recognition but also an image. When we say 'image', we refer to a collection of mental associations. At the beginning of a brand's life cycle, image relates to a number of highly tangible advantages (the key differentiating features of the product which the brand represents), but over time it begins to acquire additional intangible values (what type of consumer do we associate with the product?, what lifestyle?, what mindset?, what values?). Nike, for example, conjures up images of the United States, athletes, excellence, exertion, individuality and power. In short, the brand acquires meanings which go beyond a simple description of the product and its benefits: the brand now possesses its own independent values.

This is why it is always a serious mistake for brand names to be descriptive. Descriptive names restrict the brand's ability to break free of the real world and enter the domain of the imaginary. Fanta and Tango are better names for an orange-based soft drink than Orangina. After all, the purpose of a brand is not to describe but to differentiate the object. British consumers are familiar with the Tango product and its advertising, and are therefore well aware that it is an orangeade. However, its exotic name, with its connotations of Latin spirit and dancing, gives it an original personality which Orangina intrinsically lacks. This same logic makes Apple an inspired choice of name for a brand of user-friendly microcomputers: conventional thinking dictates that any US West Coast computer engineer should have called the company 'California Computers'. Instead, the name Apple gave the brand the ability to communicate its distinctiveness on a level which transcended physical and material considerations and the basic advantages of the actual product.

An analysis of the traditional life cycle of brands thus reveals a move away from the absolute towards the abstract… from the tangible to the intangible. In this respect, it has much in common with accountancy, which records purchases of brands as intangible assets on company balance sheets. Viewed from this perspective, a brand genuinely does add value.

Added value means a higher price. In fact, one way of calculating the financial value of a brand is to conduct research into the price differential a consumer would be ready to pay over and above the cost of an identical but unbranded (or 'unknown brand') product, or the royalty rate a company would be willing to pay for use of that brand name on one of its products.

From brand to product

In the early 1990s, the French TF1 television channel launched the successful *Ushuaïa* programme. The show was presented by the intrepid young explorer Nicholas Hulot and took the television viewer over the waterfalls of the Zambezi river aboard a microlight aircraft and across the Mekong Delta on jet skis. The show expanded beyond its original once-a-month schedule to become a weekly staple for millions of viewers, young and old alike. *Ushuaïa* had become a focal point for anyone interested in nature, escapism, 'real' life and a natural, modern outlook; in other words, the exact opposite of the 'stay-at-home', inward-looking mentality. *Ushuaïa* was a name pregnant with its own symbolism and values, and thus a potential source of value.

These factors prompted TF1 to start making active approaches to companies who would potentially be prepared to pay royalties in exchange for concession rights to the name. At around this time, the L'Oréal group was attempting to penetrate the market for shower gel, bath and deodorant products against competition from Unilever and Henkel. In these FMCG markets, each percentage point of market share is highly significant, and late arrivals face a genuine handicap. L'Oréal saw brand potential in the 'ready-to-use' *Ushuaïa* name, which not only offered a different promise from that of all existing brands in the market but also came with a strong national reputation and image. L'Oréal therefore wasted no time in licensing the name for use in the 'hygiene and beauty' sector in exchange for royalties of around 10 per cent of gross turnover.

All that was left was to come up with some products. Starting with the intrinsic meaning of the *Ushuaïa* brand, L'Oréal's marketing department produced a set of guideline specifications for its laboratories: it was now a question of creating products which complied with the spirit of this promise while generating the required profits for the business, its shareholders and its distributors.

In short, the usual cycle of a product generating a brand is succeeded by a new style of management in which the brand comes before the product. In licensing, the value must be discovered before it can be given a physical form. In brand extension, it must be first built in a specific category.

This has become the dominant management method for brands seeking to grow in mature markets. Rather than conducting 'trench warfare' campaigns between a limited number of competitors in markets where growth has all but stagnated, brands are seeking to make use of a 'lever': the renown of their own name.

Both the Virgin and Nike systems operate in this way. What is Virgin? It is an 'added value' brand which looks for the markets in which its values will be most profitably employed. What are these values? Virgin stands for irreverent, individual, freedom-loving youth. Consequently, the group seeks out all markets in which these values are important: as a world brand, Virgin enjoys the competitive advantage of recognition. This is why Virgin targets markets which are controlled by cartels or which operate under the pseudo-competitive environment of a duopoly: there is potentially a good profit to be made in these markets by a 'spoilsport' player who sabotages the tacit agreement and day-to-day equilibrium between the existing parties. As an aside, we should note that these values are all contained within the original products or events which accompanied the birth of the brand: Virgin Records was an independent record label, and Virgin Music was a mail-order record company. Therefore, instead of conducting consumer research, companies pondering their own identity would do better to look within themselves and examine their founding products (prototypes) for the key components of their mission to the marketplace.

Which are the markets identified by Virgin as pseudo-competitive, and thus a ripe environment for the genuine added value symbolized by its brand and given a tangible form by new services and liberatingly competitive products and prices? One is the cola market, dominated by Coca-Cola and Pepsi-Cola; others include the markets for sparkling orange drinks (controlled by Fanta and Orangina), vodka, credit (in the UK, where traditional banks have damaged their public reputations by charging exorbitant interest rates) and transatlantic air travel. The list of potential markets is clearly endless.

When seen from a traditional management perspective, it seems economic nonsense to set up a group which runs an airline, soft drinks and spirits companies and a bank, as well as the recent addition of a railway network operating out of London, to say nothing of its Megastore record stores and its record label. After all, we might say there was no synergy between them. But Richard Branson, who personifies the brand, sees things differently. Each of the operations is an independent company. The only overall synergy between them is created by the brand itself, which remains faithful to its contract in each market.

Another criticism raised by traditional management is the group's inexperience (and thus lack of legitimacy) in these new markets. Richard Branson's answer would be that all you need to set up a banking business is to headhunt the best banker in London and arm him with the unique asset of the Virgin name and the popular confidence which it inspires. Strength is thus combined with strength. Today, the new rationale is one of alliance. N Hayek turned to Mercedes for the automotive know-how to create a vehicle which would embody the Swatch concept. In France, Virgin Sodas went into partnership with Teisseire, the biggest national name in the concentrated fruit drinks market, in order to take advantage of its sales force and knowledge of the distribution network.

Brands without production

Brand management in its purest form is able to dispense with the production of goods altogether. What is Nike's business? It is to increase the value of the Nike brand. To do this, it must maintain the creativity of its products (by accelerating the rate of renewal) and the creativity of its advertising, and continue to focus on the stars of the 21st century world media which is sport. Nike's influence now extends to cover all sports: from its origins in running shoes, the last European Cup saw it challenge Adidas's dominant (and indeed supreme) position in the world of football. Meanwhile, the brand made inroads into the golf world by buying the services of Tiger Woods, the Mozart of world golf. Soon it will be the turn of sailing, or of skiing…

We should not forget that Nike actually manufactures nothing. It designs, presents, controls, distributes and publicizes, but does not actually produce. Nike is selling Nike, and that is all.

There is nothing new about this concept. Nike has drawn its inspiration from another master brand: Lacoste, born on the courts of Wimbledon and the French Open. The Lacoste brand was built on the success of its famous shirt, yet the company never actually manufactured the shirt itself, nor indeed any of its brand extensions. Instead, it appointed other talented companies as trusted manufacturing partners as it expanded into other, fashionable sports (such as golf and sailing), shoes, perfume, ready-to-wear fashion, sunglasses, fine leather goods, and so on. It is a licence, pure and simple. What we should remember is that Lacoste exercised control over creativity, quality and distribution to feed its own image. As a worldwide brand, it focused on the key principle of maintaining its own authenticity and ethics, two values taking their cues from sport and the colourful René Lacoste himself, and preserved over time by the discreet yet effective family management of this eponymous brand. The company grew through brand licensing, after careful scrutiny of each extension against the contract between the brand and its target market. It is this contract which forms the long-term value of a brand.

thirty one

The radicalization of design

At the last international motor show of the 20th century, there was no mistaking the importance played by design in the industry's latest models. All the major manufacturers were trying to be more innovative than their rivals, not only in respect of their showcase or concept cars, but also the more affordable models aimed at the various income brackets of the general market.

Analysts attribute this design 'revival' to several factors. An improved economic climate has made people want to go out and buy again and has put 'pleasure' firmly back on the agenda. Peugeot had already anticipated this trend in 1997 when it adopted our new brand slogan: '*Pour que l'automobile soit toujours un plaisir*' ('Making cars an everlasting pleasure'). It is a recognized fact that cars, in spite of their disadvantages and inherent costs, continue to command a high level of commitment and unfailing emotional involvement. They are the modern extension of the horse: a symbol of freedom.

Postmodern society also lends itself to this fascination for design and distinctive forms. In a fragmented society whose basic needs are satisfied, consumers are looking for – and creating – their own particular meaning. They are turning increasingly towards imaginative products which reflect their own personal values and aesthetic choices, which are no longer required to conform to a particular standard. Today, people are creating their own lifestyle and are looking beyond design to a 'concept car' that reflects their imaginary ideal. This explains the slow decline of the family saloon

Figaro Economie, 23 October 2000

in favour of 'people carriers', 4 x 4s and land-cruisers, an area in which the imagination's only limits are the existence of a well-supplied market.

It is interesting that, from the manufacturers' point of view, the obsessive concern with trying to please all of the people all of the time has survived. The average man or woman has ceased to exist. Wanting to please everyone, or at least not offend anyone, leads to the production of good all-round but mediocre models which don't fire anybody's imagination. It then takes all the skill of the dealer networks to achieve the impossible.

In addition to the above reasons, it is important to stress the key role played by 'platforms' in the modern car industry. It should be remembered that, to reduce manufacturing costs, today's multi-brand groups have several different brand models produced by the same platform, which means that these models have at least 65 per cent of their components in common. The challenge is therefore to 'type' the models – externally, internally and even in terms of the driving experience – sufficiently well to make consumers forget about platforms and focus on brand identity. The alternative is to risk falling into the 'cannibalization' trap, as in the case of the Passat estate, which is very similar to the much more expensive Audi estate, a fact that Volkswagen dealers never fail to point out to prospective customers. However, multi-brand logic aims to maximize market coverage by emphasizing brand differentiation.

Given the openness between sections and departments, and the policy of common platforms, there is an almost in-built tendency towards imitation within the same manufacturing group. This results in resemblances when the very essence of branding is in fact differentiation, which is why design is now being used to emphasize perceived differences. In this way, the 'platform' policy is directly responsible for the radicalization of design.

The question then arises as to the nature of the design, and a major consideration comes into play. Brand differentiation cannot be based solely on appearances and different 'looks'. A properly constructed brand portfolio only makes long-term sense if it contains innovative brands inspired by different values, to which a large section of the general public may aspire even though they may not necessarily subscribe.

It is revealing that the key word in modern brand management is no longer image but identity, ie the value system specific to each brand. In our postmodern age, even if loyalty can no longer be taken for granted and consumers have to be repeatedly wooed and won over with the launch of each new model, the fact remains that the consumer's allegiance to and affinity with a particular brand is sustained by these values.

Values also play a key role within the overall brand structure. Since the brand is a long-term landmark, only these values can help maintain a sense of direction: by defining the product plan, directing the search for new ideas and structuring the advertising for each individual brand. In today's marketplace, it is no longer a question of challenging brand values, but of understanding how each of these values should be expressed and updated to meet constantly evolving consumer taste.

Brand values are therefore essential for designers. In addition to the models that target a particular market segment, it is also important to convey the brand identity and its values. The trend is therefore towards a form of symbolic design: a 'de-sign'. Modern design is undoubtedly at the service of form and function, but is above all responsible for externalizing the internal driving force of any brand, ie its intrinsic mission.

Conclusion

Breaking free of the herd mentality

Today, every company wants its own brand. Battles are being waged between producers and distributors in the name of brand promotion. The same is true of manufacturers of components and finished products: again, the name of the game is to generate value. This is hardly surprising: we brand, therefore we are.

At a time when the old leaders are vanishing and traditional distinctions are becoming blurred, brands themselves are inspiring the alliances of the future. A brand's power lies in its ability to form relationships with its customers. This is neatly summed up by the US term 'bonding'. The bond forged by a belief in the product's exclusivity, superiority or image creates not just customers, but an unshakeable community of adepts. The issue at stake goes beyond loyalty: it is one of mutual commitment. The ultimate aim of all brands is to create a unique, unbreakable bond of this kind. In tomorrow's market, who will be best placed to cement these bonds? The great strength of the distributor is its broad horizontal base. Its extensive cross-category purchasing databases provide the perfect tool for segmentation, identifying relationships between the sales of brands as diverse as Evian, Pampers and Nivea. This extremely precise targeting device now puts the distributor in a stronger position than ever before to manipulate demand; and demand is easy enough to manipulate.

The distributor's influence and structural insight is counterbalanced by another type of relationship – in this case, of the emotional, aspirational kind. Despite their increasing market share and level of exposure, distributor brands are purchased for reasons of pragmatism rather than emotional involvement. Consumers may buy Tesco yogurts, but only as a 'second-best' substitute for Yoplait or Danone. This is the sort of bond that manufacturers must learn to forge and maintain. It thrives on the strength of the specialist's considerable expertise in products, services, communication and – most importantly – ideas. A brand can retain its aspirational qualities only if it continues to change and reinvent itself.

Local brands also have proximity on their side: they benefit from the remarkable advantage of cultural familiarity, and need only ensure that their efficiency and service remain up to date. For this reason, and contrary to received wisdom, we do not believe in the 'single model' of brand. Consumer diversity calls for brand diversity. If we unduly restrict the number of brands in the shops, just as if we were restricting the number of political parties, we reject the market economy in favour of totalitarianism.

However, one thing is certain: in the future, all remaining competitors will be excellent. Implementation considerations will thus become all important. A strategy's merits will be judged by how it is put into practice.

In the light of increasingly uniform quality among the surviving products in the consumer arena, it will become vital to emphasize the brand's value system, the aspirational engine which drives the development of new product. After all, technically speaking, a Peugeot is as good as an Audi or a Volkswagen. What matters are not so much the physical characteristics of the cars each brand produces, but the deep-rooted automotive values, history and philosophy each represents. Peugeot's car vision is not the same as Volkswagen's, much less Renault's.

Postmodern consumers may buy budget cars, but they still require signs, meaning and a reflection of their own identity. In the car market, which is fragmenting itself into a myriad of new expectations, only the clearest brand values will be capable of pointing managers towards the new sectors in which the brand can freely express its distinctive values to the greatest profit.

All too often, companies are guilty of conducting only token research into the brand's identity: yet such research is necessary to an understanding of how to adapt to a constantly changing environment. Without an understanding of the brand's inner values, we are at the mercy of the 'herd mentality' approaches of brand image surveys and lifestyle research. A brand with no concept of its own identity is left with no alternative but to chase vainly after the latest fads and trends.

We must replace conformity and the 'herd mentality' with the philosophy of the brand. After all, a brand's strength is built upon its determination to promote its own distinctive values, and mission.

References

Abell, D (1993) *Managing with Dual Strategies*, Free Press, New York

Boisdévésy, J-C (1996) *Le Marketing Relationnel*, Éditions d'Organisation, Paris

Christensen, C (1999) *The Innovator's Dilemma*, Harvard University Press, Boston, MA

Collins, J and Porras, J (1994) *Built to Last*, Harper Business, New York

Ehrenberg, A (1972) *Repeat Buying*, 2nd edn, Edward Arnold, London

Godin, S (1999) *Permission Marketing*, Simon & Schuster, New York

Hartley, R (1998) *Marketing Mistakes*, Wiley, London

Kapferer, J-N (1991) *Rumors*, Transaction Publishers, New Brunswick.

Kapferer, J-N and Laurent, G (1995) *La Sensibilité aux Marques*, Éditions d'Organisation, Paris

Kapferer, J-N and Laurent, G (1998) *Comment les consommateurs perçoivent-ils les méga-marques*, HEC research report

Kniebihler, M and Giaoui, F (1998) *L'automobile sans concession*, Éditions d'Organisation, Paris

Laurent, G, Kapferer, J-N and Roussel, F (1990) The underlying structure of brand awareness scores, *Marketing Science*, **14** (3), pp 170–79

Lenz, V (1999) *The Saturn Difference*, John Wiley and Sons, New York

Lewi, C and Kapferer, J-N (1998) Consumers' preference for retailers' brands. Esoman Proceedings.

Macrae, C (1996) *The Brand Chartering Handbook*, Addison-Wesley, London
Morgan, A (1998) *Eating the Big Fish*, Adweek Book, New York
Pointillart, H and Xardel, D (1996) *Mégabases*, Village Mondial, Paris
Rapp, S and Collins, L (1994) *Beyond Maxi-Marketing*, McGraw-Hill, New York
Raypont, J and Sviokla, J (1994) Managing in the marketspace, *Harvard Business Review*, **72** (6), p 141
Rechenmann, J-J (1999) *l'Internet et le Marketing*, Éditions d'Organisation, Paris
Reichheld, F (1996) *The Loyalty Effect*, Harvard Business School Press, Boston, MA
Rosen, E (2000) *The Anatomy of Buzz*, HarperCollins Business, London
Seybold, P (1998) *Customers.com*, Times Business, New York
Sicard, M-C (1998) *La Métamorphose des Marques*, Éditions d'Organisation, Paris
Slywotzky, A (1998) *Value Migration*, Village Mondial, Paris
Slywotzky, A and Morrison, D (1999) *La Zone de Profit*, Village Mondial, Paris
Tharoor, S (1997) *India – From midnight to the Millennium*, Harper, London
Trout, J and Rivkin, S (1999) *The New Positioning*, McGraw-Hill, New York
Zyman, S (1999) *The End of Marketing as We Know it*, HarperCollins, New York

Index

NB: numbers in italics indicate drawings, figures, graphs or tables